Dedication

I am eternally grateful to my grandfather
Johannis Aaltsz, in whose shadow I plodded as a three-year-old
and who gave me a lasting love for the living earth.
To him I dedicate this book.

The author aged 4 years

Gardening with Young Children

Beatrys Lockie

Hawthorn Press

Published by Hawthorn Press, Hawthorn House, 1 Lansdown Lane, Stroud, Gloucestershire, GL5 1BJ, UK
Tel: (01453) 757040 Fax: (01453) 751138
info@hawthornpress.com   www.hawthornpress.com

Cover photograph by Dr. James D. Lockie
Illustrations © Fred Cannon and Alma Dowle
Photographs by Dr. James D. Lockie
Cover design by Hawthorn Press, Stroud, Gloucestershire
Design and typesetting by Lynda Smith at Hawthorn Press, Stroud, Gloucestershire
Printed in the UK by The Cromwell Press, Trowbridge, Wiltshire

Mixed Sources
Product group from well-managed forests and other controlled sources
www.fsc.org Cert no. TT-TOC-2082
© 1996 Forest Stewardship Council
FSC

Lines from *The Seed Shop*, Muriel Stuart, reprinted by permission of Mrs Elizabeth Stapleforth. An extract on earthworms from *Soil and Civilisation*, Edward Hyams, 1952 reprinted by kind permission of Thames and Hudson Ltd. 'The Song of the Hawthorn Fairy', 'Song of the Horsechestnut Fairy', 'Song of the Acorn Fairy', from *Flower Fairies of the Autumn*, Cicely Mary Barker, the Estate of Cicely Mary Barker, 1926, 1944 reprinted by permission of Frederick Warne and Company. 'The Song of the May Fairy' from *Flower Fairies of the Spring*, Cicely Mary Barker, the Estate of Cicely Mary Barker, 1926, 1944 reprinted by permission of Frederick Warne and Company. 'The Song of the Self Heal Fairy' from *Flower Fairies of the Wayside* by Cicely Mary Barker, the Estate of Cicely Mary Barker, 1948 reprinted by Frederick Warne and Company. 'My Nice Red Rosy Apple', from *Festivals, Family and Food*, Diana Carey and Judy Large, 1982 reprinted by kind permission of Hawthorn Press. 'One day when we went walking', Janine Hobbs from *The Horn Book Magazine,* January 1947, reprinted by permission of The Horn Book Inc., Boston. MA.   www.hbook.com

Every effort has been made to trace the ownership of all copyrighted material. If any omission has been made, please bring this to the publisher's attention so that proper acknowledgment may be given in future editions.

British Library Cataloguing in Publication Data applied for

ISBN 978-1-903458-38-9

Contents

List of Poems and Songs

Acknowledgements

I gratefully acknowledge the kind permission of the following authors to use extracts from their work: M. Myerkort, Steiner Kindergarten teacher, ('Summer Goodbye'); Charles Kovacs, Steiner teacher, ('Rainy Weather'); Eileen Hutchins, Steiner kindergarten teacher ('Mother Earth'); and all Steiner kindergarten teachers who have built up and maintained a wealth of poems, songs and stories which have become traditional: 'The Gift of Light' from the Advent Garden, 'The Story of the Christmas Rose', 'How the Snowdrop Got its Colour'. A huge thank you to my husband, James, not only for typing but also for his continued encouragement. Without his help this book would not have happened.

Preface

This is a first principle book for those teaching tomorrow's gardeners. Starting appropriately with the autumn, Beatrys Lockie follows a lively, imaginative and yet practical path through a child's experience of a growing year in a country garden, emphasising the whole round of nature and its relationship with both the immediate and the larger environment.

The journey embraces the organic garden archetype right through to the city garden and gardening in containers for those who have no natural soil resource, and even suggests making chutney from vegetables and fruit. Music, song and story enliven the growing activity and its festivals. A whole range of insect, bird and mammal vistas broaden the view to include key relationships between animal, plant and soil. Many practical exercises are woven in to fire teachers' or parents' ideas and enthusiasm. All this is in harmony with the seasons, and central are the elements of earth, air, fire and water and the warm compost heap. Plant awareness, fertility management and seed-saving encourage care and sustainability. Beatrys Lockie's magic understanding of young children's feeling and doing connection with nature is clearly evident throughout.

This book comes at a time when we adults increasingly struggle to manage our fragile environment sensitively and bear responsibility for it. And so, perhaps, this is a new beginning which reminds us of the age-old wisdom: 'Except we become as little children...'

Jimmy Anderson, M.B.E.
(formerly Soil Association)

About this Book

This book is meant to be used by anyone who plays, works with and guides children between the ages of three and seven: kindergarten teachers, playgroup leaders, parents and child-minders. While some of this book may be read like a kindergarten guide, obviously everything that is presented here can easily be adapted for one or more children in the home and elsewhere, and for various lengths of time. If, for example you are looking after, or working with children throughout the day, then they will certainly need a quiet rest period between the morning and afternoon.

One does not usually associate three-year-olds with gardening and yet, why not? Isn't this the age when they cannot help but imitate, when they feel happiest being active and when they are wide-open to ideas properly presented?

'Properly presented' is the crux of the matter because the small child's consciousness is very different from that of the adult. Small children experience no borderline between their own being and the outside world; they are at one with the world around them. Just watch and listen to a three-year-old speaking to a lamb, puppy or kitten. He[*] is at one with the animal and treats it as though it were part of himself or, at least, an equal. The small child lives in a world of pictures and images. Ideas can only properly be accepted by young children if you appeal to their feeling; and this is done by presenting the idea through a story which conjures vivid images, feeding the child's soul. For this reason, those who deal with small children must always strive to create these pictures anew for them so that they may enter into the mood rather than just the facts of the story. If you doubt the power stories have for children, just watch them as an experienced story-teller gets to

---

[*] I have used the male form only to avoid awkwardness of expression. The reader is invited, of course, to imagine both boys and girls.

work. I can remember many instances of even difficult children being captivated by a story well told. One in particular, nick-named 'hell on wheels' by the local community, was brought to silent, wide-eyed awe as the story progressed. Every story begins with a ritual: first the candle is lit, then a little bell is rung and finally, 'Can I hear a pin drop? – Now we can begin.' One should not over-dramatise stories for young children as they can easily become over-excited. Dramatisation really belongs to a later stage of childhood.

Many grown-ups, by contrast, live in a world of the intellect, of logical cause and effect. This is foreign territory for a small child. The child can make little of this approach, and quickly becomes bored. Worst of all, a child fed nothing but intellectual fodder can later become emotionally stunted. An intellectual adult often finds it more difficult to conjure vivid images than does a more intuitive person. But we can all try. Otherwise, what we give to children goes right over their heads. In order to help with this I have, here and there in the text, suggested how one might put an idea across to the small child. This is not talking down to either the adult reader or the child but is rather an attempt to present ideas in a way that is in tune with the child's mental and emotional development.

Young children have a natural sense of wonder. It is up to us to cultivate and nurture this by showing them how to hold things carefully, especially living things, answer their questions in an imaginative, friendly and open way, show them your awe of nature, and talk to plants and embrace trees. Let them feel gratitude for all weathers, not just those that suit us, and teach them to love everything. As Satish Kumar, the founder of *Resurgence* magazine, once said on a radio programme: 'Every weather is beautiful!'

Working with young children is an awesome responsibility because they soak up all that comes their way, whether good, bad, or indifferent. We have to try to convey what is good and wholesome, all that is caring and moral. The stories, poems and songs in this book aim to help create such a mood.

Ritual before storytelling:

Lighting the candle

'Can I hear a pin drop?'

CHAPTER 1

Some Down-to-Earth Facts to Begin

Soil Acidity

Soil is the basis of any garden. The better the soil, the better the prospects of growing lots of different plants and growing them well. Understanding the type of soil you have is vital to your choosing the best plants to grow. Soils may be acid (sour), alkaline (sweet) or in between (neutral). In chemistry, acid and alkaline liquids are measured on a scale of 1-10 and this measurement is called the pH. So, when we refer to the pH of a soil we are simply referring to its acidity or alkalinity. A value of pH 5.5 is very acid, pH 6.5 is slightly acid, pH 7 is neutral, and pH 7.5 slightly alkaline.

You can test your soil with a cheap kit bought from a garden centre. It is a lovely thing to do with the children and the changing colour is like magic. You can practise first by making an acid solution with water and a little white vinegar in a small clear bottle, then the same with plain water and finally with baking soda in water (alkaline). Add the solution provided in the kit. Each liquid will assume a different colour and the pH can be read off for each by comparing it with a chart provided. Now, collect some soil from just below the surface of your garden and put a little in the clear bottle and add the pH testing liquid. Shake it up and allow to settle. The colour of the liquid is compared with the colour chart and the degree of acidity read off. If you can get some litmus paper, it is even more magical for the children. You simply make a solution with water and soil and allow it to settle. Then put the litmus paper in. It will change colour before your eyes. Of course, you do not bother the children with pH readings and all that. Sweet, sour and in-between soil, and the colours of each, are enough.

Ideally, soil should be about pH 6.5, i.e. slightly acid, because this is the soil that most plants like. But, rhododendrons, azaleas and potatoes do best in an acid soil of about pH 5.5. By contrast, the cabbage family, fuchsias, pinks and alliums prefer alkaline conditions (pH 7.5).

Plant Preferences

Most plants live within a pH range which can be quite wide. Here are some of the ranges of pH that common flowers, shrubs and vegetables can tolerate. You may have to modify the soil in pot or garden in order to give particular plants the best conditions to thrive.

- Potato, rhododendron and azalea, blue hydrangea, lily of the valley, blackberry (bramble): pH 4-6.
- Apple, raspberry, viola, fuchsia, holly: pH 5-6.5.
- Sunflower, parsley, strawberry, carrot, aubretia, honeysuckle, hyacinth, petunia, sweetpea, beans (broad, French and runner), cabbage family, kale, spinach, radish, lettuce: pH 6-7.5.
- Leek, geranium, snowdrop, watercress, convolvulus, white hydrangea, some mosses, wisteria: pH 6-8.
- Mint, paprika: pH 7-8.5.

If your garden is very alkaline because the underlying rock is chalky, you can change it a little, locally, by adding compost which is usually a little bit acid, or peat. Peat is of two main sorts: 'fen peat' (for example from the Norfolk Broads) is slightly alkaline; and 'bog peat' from upland bogs is very acidic. Bog peat covers enormous areas of the uplands and may reach a depth of 5m (16') or more. It is composed mainly of sphagnum moss with some sedges and grasses. It forms the basis for some ericacious composts (for growing rhododendrons, potatoes and heathers) and needs the addition of lime to make it useable for most plants requiring a pH of just under or just over 7. There are, currently, anxieties at the speed with which peat reserves are being used up not only for gardens but also for firing electricity stations, for example, in Ireland. This has led to the production of alternatives to peat for use in horticulture based on coconut fibre or leaf mould, both of which have similar characteristics to real peat. You should chose the alternatives whenever possible; the source will be marked on the bag you get in the garden centre. If your garden is too acid (as in some town gardens or in peaty areas), you can raise the pH locally by adding some hydrated lime (available from garden centres). But if your soil is extreme, you may have to accept what you have and plan your garden accordingly.

If you are lucky to have a soil of pH 6.5, you can modify it a bit either way in order to grow a wider range of plants. Rhododendrons, azaleas, heathers and potatoes prefer a pH of 5.5 and this can be obtained with peat, compost and locally, ericaceous compost. Cabbages, kale, broccoli and fuchsias prefer a pH of 7.5 and this can be obtained by adding hydrated lime.

Soil Structure

Soil structure is also important and you should identify whether you have a sandy, chalky, clayey, soil or a mixture of these types.

- Sandy soils are light and easy to work. They are free-draining and so are liable to dry out and to lose nutrients. You must, therefore, keep on adding organic matter in order to increase the 'body' of the soil and to retain moisture.

- Chalky soils are derived from limestone and are shallow and lacking body. Like sandy soils, they need lots and lots of organic matter.
- Clay soils are usually fertile but they are very heavy to work and when they dry out they become hard and cracked. You can modify them by adding organic material, grit and sharp sand in order to break up the clay and let air in.
- Loamy soils are the ideal. They have a good balance of organic material as humus, and sand and some clay. They are free-draining, well aerated, rich in nutrients and retain moisture well And, what is more, they are easily worked. Even loam soils can become exhausted and so the gardener must keep them in good heart by adding manures and composts regularly (see p.83).

Collect examples of the different kinds of soil: peat, sandy, clay and loam. Let the children feel the differences between them. It is pretty obvious why clay is the only one suitable for making pots. Test all the types of soil for their pH.

Weather

Whether the weather be fine,
Or whether the weather be not,
Whether the weather be cold,
Or whether the weather be hot,
We'll weather the weather, whatever the weather,
Whether we like it or not.

Anon

Weather is important in gardening not just for the gardener's comfort but also for that of the plants. Weather forecasts give a general account but local variations are far more important. If you do not know about your local weather, ask other gardeners nearby.

What is the height above sea-level of your garden? Average temperature falls off as you rise higher. Do you suffer from late and early frosts and therefore have to protect frost-sensitive plants into late spring? Are you sheltered from cold winds in spring? Do you live in a

'frost hollow'? All these aspects can be dealt with by providing suitable temporary or permanent shelter.

Shelter from winds and frost is important. Cold winds can blister and kill young seedlings or, at least, give them such a fright that they never fully recover. You can make a permanent hedge to break the prevailing wind by using willow cuttings which are plentiful in marshy areas and by streams (see 'Propagation' p.100), or you may use evergreen shrubs bought in or propagated from your own shrubs. As a more temporary measure, you can use 1m-high chicken netting (wire netting with a 2.5cm [1″] hole) stretched between stakes driven into the ground. This, like willows in winter when there are no leaves, will not stop the wind but it will filter it so that it loses much of its sting. You can also protect individual plants with milk cartons or clear plastic bottles with the bottom cut off and the cap removed and used as 'cloches', or with straw or newspaper.

How to Fit Gardening into a Full Schedule

You may ask how you can possibly fit gardening into an already apparently full schedule. Most groups meet for about three hours every weekday morning and the following is how I fitted gardening into my week. One must, of course, be flexible: some days are pelting with rain and are unsuitable for outdoor activities. In that case, do something inside and save up some time for gardening later. Or do a few minutes of gardening preparation in readiness for the time when you can go out.

09.30-09.45	Free play until all are assembled.
09.45-10.00	Ring time.
10.00-10.30	The day's work.
10.30-11.00	Snack time.
11.00-11.30	Walk, outside play, gardening.
11.30-12.00	Tidying away and story time.
12.00-12.30	Free play.

Gardening sometimes takes only ten minutes of the half hour; at other times the whole half hour can be used. And gardening can be done every day in the week or on set days. If the latter, it is best to keep as far as possible to specific days so that a routine develops and the children have a point or points in the week to look forward to.

If you spend as little as ten minutes on gardening then you really have to be well organised for otherwise the ten minutes is spent looking for tools and deciding what to do. I always kept the tools where we could find them easily (it is a part of the children's tidying up to put the tools where they can be found again) and they know to bring wellies on gardening days. I also primed them by talking briefly beforehand about what we would be doing so that their interest is aroused. And, of course, there are gardening jobs such as practising sowing (see p.75) and sowing in pots (see p.64) that can be done indoors.

My gardening week went something like this, always allowing for variations due to bad weather, or different seasons:

Day 1   Weeds out (p.78).
Day 2   Treading the paths (p.69).
Day 3   Planting (p.70); I have the plants ready.
Day 4   Planting seedlings from inside sowing (p.72).
Day 5   Sowing new plants and vegetables (p.74).

CHAPTER 2.

Autumn

Why Begin in Autumn?

Many people think of starting with the garden in spring. Certainly, spring is the time of new growth. However, spring growth needs preparation and that begins in autumn. I have always found that preparation in everything you do pays dividends and it is part of the whole cycle.

Preparation includes preparing the ground by weeding, removing big stones, and mulching and manuring. Autumn is the time for harvesting what you have grown the previous summer. It is also the time to prepare for winter festivals such as Advent, Christmas and New Year. And, after that, the snowdrops will be out and spring is not far off.

What happens in autumn? The usual answer is that plants are dying and the flowers and leaves are shrivelling and falling off. Some plants, the annuals, do indeed die and grow again each year from seed; and others, the biennials, die every second year. However most, the perennials, do not really die, but go for a long sleep during the cold winter weather. And just as children go to sleep at night and waken up in the morning so plants will waken again in spring. They are very much alive, especially under the ground where their roots are protected.

Give the children an imaginative, fairy-tale picture of what is happening underground in winter. For instance:

Sparkles underground

Underground it is not as dark as you might expect. It is lit up with a thousand little stars all shining and twinkling. Gnomes are working deep under the earth with their little axes and hammers. They break the stones and release the minerals that plants need and take up by their roots; and they release the crystals inside the stones for human beings to use and enjoy.

(Have crystals on hand for the children to see and hold.)

Gnomes working underground

Now, gather the children around you and starting with the obviously wrong season, ask them:

Is it spring time?
No
Is it summer time?
No
What then?
It is autumn time.

With as many beautiful gestures as you can muster, teach them their first song.

Summer goodbye, summer goodbye,   *(waving goodbye)*
You can no longer stay.
Autumn will chase you away.   *(chasing gesture)*
Summer goodbye, summer goodbye.

M. Myerkort

Sum – mer good – bye, sum – mer good – bye,

You can no lon – g - er stay. Aut – umn will chase you a - way.

Sum – mer good – bye, sum – mer good – bye.

Gestures

Using gestures when telling a story

Gestures are important. Children naturally move their whole body, and gestures are a large part of their communication. A great deal is acquired through imitation. It is therefore important that the child always sees appropriate and meaningful gestures. If, for example, the teacher uses gentle gestures to put, say, a doll in its cradle, the children will unerringly imitate the gestures. Unfortunately, through the influence of some television programmes, children's gestures can become wild, jagged, stereotyped and meaningless. On the whole, it is best to play things down and not to exaggerate. Use gestures while telling stories, singing songs and in plays. Some examples are given in the text alongside stories and songs.

The hand-shake is also a gesture. It gives the teacher a good idea of the state of the children when they arrive in the morning. Does the child's hand feel the same as yesterday? Is the hand unusually cold or warm? Is the hand-shake uncertain or overdone? These signs tell the teacher something that can perhaps be used to support the child.

Autumn's Seeds are Next Year's Plants

Seeds come in all shapes and sizes. At one extreme, as in willows, they are tiny with no food reserves and so have to germinate as soon as shed: at the other extreme the coconut has enormous food reserves to carry it over until it can become established on a sandy beach hundreds of miles from where it was dropped. Some seeds, like broom, have tough skins that water has difficulty in penetrating. So the seeds lie in the ground and are rubbed by grit which wears the skin and lets water in and growth begins. Some seeds need special frost treatment before they can grow in Spring. Other seeds, such as hawthorn, germinate after they have passed through a bird and these seeds have attractively coloured fruity coverings that birds like to eat. That is why you often find a scattering of hawthorns on hillsides in southern Scotland and of rowans in Highland Scotland. Fieldfares and other thrushes have deposited them there complete with a pellet of fertiliser.

The Song of the Hawthorn Fairy

These thorny branches bore the May
So many months ago,
That when the scattered petals lay
Like drifts of fallen snow,
'This is the stories end,' you said;
But, O, not half was told!
For see, my haws are here instead,
And hungry birdies shall be fed
On these when days are cold.

Cicely Mary Barker

Pine and Fir Cones as Weather Indicators

Trees like pine, spruce and fir have cones which open to shed seed when the air is dry and the weather fine and the seed can best disperse; but shut tightly when the air around is wet. You can try this with the children by hanging cones inside and outside. In a warmish room they will open quite quickly. Outside they will begin to open as good weather approaches, and close as bad weather comes, thus acting as little weather indicators.

Pine cones closed and open

Other seeds, like rose-bay willow herb (fireweed), thistles, and dandelions have a little parachute that lets the seed drift for miles in the wind. This is why waste ground is so quickly colonised by these plants. Sycamore and ash seeds have a wing that acts like a helicopter, taking the seed on the wind away from the parent tree to where it has room to spread. Goldfinches and siskins eat the seeds of thistles so, if you go out to watch the thistle seeds blowing away in the wind, look out for the little birds that depend on these seeds for their food.

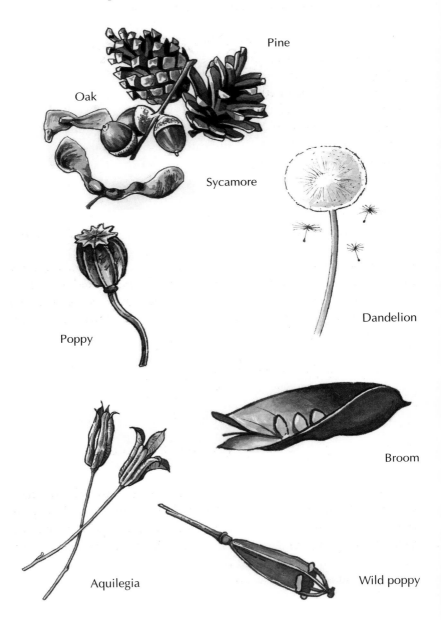

Pine

Oak

Sycamore

Dandelion

Poppy

Broom

Aquilegia

Wild poppy

Birds and mammals often help acorns from oak trees to find a good place to grow. If you live near oaks, you may see rooks and jackdaws carrying acorns into nearby fields; they eat some and bury others for later but then forget about them and the acorns grow. Squirrels hoard acorns for the winter and, like the rooks, mislay some.

The Song of the Acorn Fairy

To English folk the mighty oak
Is England's noblest tree;
Its hard-grained wood is strong and good
As English hearts can be.
And, would you know how oak-trees grow,
The secret may be told:
You do but need to plant for seed
One acorn in the mould;
For even so, long years ago,
Were born the oaks of old.

Cicely Mary Barker

All seeds have one thing in common. The germ or part that will grow into a plant is very small; the rest is food reserve and protective covering. It is a source of wonder that this tiny germ can grow into a flower or shrub or forest tree. Muriel Stuart has caught this sense of awe in the last lines of her poem 'The Seed Shop':

...sealed in their shells a thousand roses leap,
Here I can blow a garden with my breath,
And in my hand a forest lies asleep.*

Collecting and Storing Seeds

The sheer variety and beauty in a collection of seeds will stimulate interest and amazement. Gather the children around to look at your collection of seeds. Try to choose the more spectacular such as the tiny pansy which sits snugly in a cradle, and the poppy with its lovely

---

* Published in: *In the Orchard*, Kettillonia 2000.

containers; and the seeds of honesty set in their round windows. Balsam pods give you a fright when you hold them because in the warmth of a hand they explode, scattering seeds everywhere. Don't forget the various seeds we eat: wheat, oats, barley and rye, and the very different kinds of bread that each produces. And there are seeds in apples, pears, peaches and grapes. The avocado and mango have a single enormous seed.

The Song of the Horse Chestnut Fairy

My conkers they are shiny things,
And things of mighty joy,
And they are like the wealth of kings
To every little boy;
I see the upturned face of each
Who stands around the tree;
He sees his treasure out of reach
But does not notice me.

For love of conkers bright and brown,
He pelts the tree all day;
With stones and sticks he knocks them down,
And thinks it jolly play.
But sometimes I, the elf, am hit
Until I'm black and blue;
O, laddies, only wait a bit,
I'll shake them down to you!

Cicely Mary Barker

Now, take the children out, armed with clear plastic bags, to plants with seed pods on them. Listening to the seeds rattling inside the pods and guessing what they look like is fun. You can sometimes hear the pips inside an apple, especially the apple called Cox's Orange Pippin, when you shake it. Collect seed for planting next year in the garden and window box and keep some for the bird bell (see p.38). Choose easy seeds for sowing such as poppy, heartsease (wild pansy), pansy, snapdragon and calendula (pot marigold).

Seeds are in containers of all sorts and shapes and nature knows when the seeds are dry and ready to be shed on to the ground. Later rain, wind, sun, and sometimes frost will help make them grow. We try to gather the seeds when they are just ready to be shed. This is easy with poppies which have large, beautifully shaped containers with holes through which the seed falls. With other plants, you may have to collect the seed just before it is ripe and dry it off on a sheet of paper in a warm room. As a guide to knowing when the seeds are dry, they should run off your hand like sand running through an egg timer. When quite dry, the different kinds of seed are put in separate envelopes, marked with the name and year of collection. Then, store them in a cool dry place.

And here is rhyme to be said as children cut their apple crossways.

My nice red, rosy apple
Has a secret midst unseen
You'd see if you could creep inside
Five rooms so neat and clean.
In each room there are living
Two pips so black and bright.
Asleep they are and dreaming
Of lovely warm sunlight.
And sometimes they are dreaming
Of many things to be,
How soon they will be hanging
Upon the Christmas tree.

Diana Carey and Judy Large

Making Things with Berries, Seeds and Leaves

Now we start collecting things to make ornaments from berries, pumpkin and melon seeds and leaves.

You will need: coloured thread and wool, needles and a bodkin or large needle, some corrugated packing paper, some paper clips, a paper stapler and a plant press.

A plant press is necessary to flatten and dry flowers and leaves. If you haven't got one you can improvise. You will need two sheets of hardboard and lots of sheets of absorbent paper (newspaper will do). The flowers and leaves to be dried go between sheets of absorbent paper (and dry quickly) and are weighed down by heavy books or bricks. If the leaves are fleshy, you may have to change the paper a few times. Sheets of thick pastel coloured paper are needed for making cards. Have rescue remedy and plasters ready in case of little accidents!

Flower press

Beautiful necklaces can be made from melon and pumpkin seeds and rowan berries and rose hips. The seeds are best dried on a sheet of paper so that they can be painted if you wish. The berries and rosehips are best used fresh; over time they will dry and become a little wrinkled. Thread the seeds and berries on cotton or woollen thread with a thickness appropriate to the size of the seed or berry.

Rhododendron leaves are beautiful in autumn. They are in shades of yellow, green, brown red and spotted. There are, of course, many other brightly coloured leaves, such as virginia creeper, but for a head-dress the leaves need to be strong and stiff and to have a reasonably long stalk.

To make a head-dress for the children to wear, cut the corrugated paper to the size of the head and hold a small overlap with paper clips. Then consolidate this with the stapler. You can paint the corrugated paper if you wish.

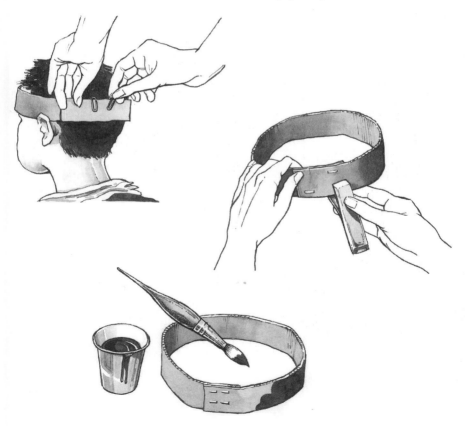

Push the stalk of each leaf into the tubes of the paper. This should be enough to hold the leaves upright and in place but, if not, a thread passed through each leaf will do. Or a touch of glue on each stalk will fix the leaves in place.

Once the leaves in the press have dried, you can stick them on thick pastel-coloured paper in all sorts of combinations and designs. These cards can be used for Christmas, with the design perhaps in the form of a star, and for birthdays. Believe me, the children will have many more ideas than you; you just have to start them off.

Bulbs, Tubers and Corms

Plants can multiply by means other than seeds: by tubers, corms and bulbs. Tubers and corms are parts of plant stems or roots that become swollen with food allowing them to root and produce a new plant. A bulb is a stem with swollen leaves and flowers pressed closely together, which you can see very plainly if you cut a bulb, like an onion or hyacinth, in two.

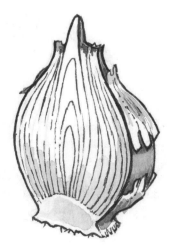

Hyacinth bulb

And, of course, many of these swollen stems we find good to eat and so we cultivate them. Examples of bulbs are: the crocus, cyclamen and onion; of the tuber, the potato; and of a corm, the iris, dahlia and begonia. Some bulbs, like those of winter aconite and cyclamen, are hard and woody. Most, however, when dormant or resting, hold moisture and are firm and plump with no shrivelling and with no black spots or other signs of mouldiness.

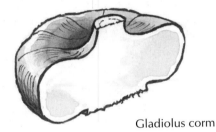

Gladiolus corm   Potato tuber

So, what is the difference between a seed and a tuber like a potato (or a corm or bulb)? It is this: a seed is produced by two parents and bears the likeness of each. Inherent in this is variability and therefore the possibility of new varieties; for example, all the different kinds of potatoes are derived from seed. The plant grower then selects a potato plant that looks promising in some way. In contrast, tubers, bulbs and corms are clones of a single plant and are therefore identical to it. This is how we can perpetuate a potato variety whereas the seed from the same plant would produce a mish-mash of potato types. So, in order to get new varieties (although most are useless) we breed two parents and collect the seed. But once we have a variety we want to keep and perpetuate, we use tubers, bulbs and corms to keep the variety true.

Here again is a concept that is, perhaps, difficult for children. We might share this with the small child by saying that seeds need a mother and father, while potatoes are like big buds from the mother potato plant.

There are other means by which plants can make more of their own kind but explanation of cuttings and layering comes later (see 'Propagation' p.100).

Planting Bulbs in Pots

Most of the bulbs planted in spring for summer and late summer flowering such as gladioli and lillies originate in warm countries. They can only be put outside when frosts are past. However, here we will only concern ourselves with hardy bulbs such as crocus, daffodil and hyacinth.

These bulbs benefit from early planting so now (autumn) is the time to get them in. You can plant them in pots for winter flowering or outside for spring flowering. The way of planting is the same for each except that in planting bulbs outside you must loosen the soil because the roots find it difficult to push through compacted soil. You will need flower pots, light soil or compost and some small stones to put in the bottom of the pot to prevent waterlogging.

This is a good moment to consider plastic versus clay pots. Plants need to breathe, not only the flowers, leaves and stalks but also the roots. Clay pots are porous: they have lots of tiny holes in them which allows air in. Plastic pots do not. Let the children also experience the different feel of plastic and clay. Get out a basin of soapy water and set them to cleaning the pots to their hearts' content (after all, you don't put babies into dirty beds, do you?).

On a certain day you can go out into a field and collect little stones to place in the bottom of the flower pots, and soil from mole heaps. Use pails and spades or even just plastic bags and hands. Don't forget to say 'Thank you' to Mr. and Mrs. Mole. Or you can buy compost in a garden centre (not so much fun).

Put stones in the bottom of your plant pot and quarter-fill with soil or compost. Press down lightly. Look carefully at the bulb: which is top and which bottom? The top has a point as if to pierce the earth and push out into the light. The bottom has a round pad from which we can easily imagine roots eventually coming. Place the crocus bulb in the pot the right way up and top up with soil or compost to twice the height of the bulb.

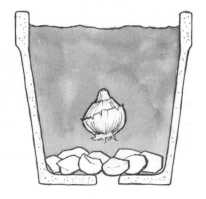

Collecting earth from mole-heaps

Spreading earth from Mr. and Mrs. Mole on a raised bed

Give the bulb a drink, just enough to moisten the soil, and place it in a cool dark place.

Now the bulbs are going to sleep just as children do at bed-time and the soil is tucked in nice and cosily like a blanket. Every week we must look at them and give them more water if they need it.

The idea is to keep the soil or compost just damp. And now close the curtains and switch off the light as we put them into a dark cupboard for their sleep.

Goodnight, sleep tight.

We can also bless the earth with a song like this one:

Mother Earth, Mother Earth, take this seed and give it birth.
Father Sun, gleam and glow, make it warm and let it grow.
Sister Rain, Sister Rain, shed your tears to swell the grain.
Brother Wind, breathe and blow, so that the leaves green may grow.

Eileen Hutchins

The Autumn Harvest

Now comes another important part of the autumn work. It is the harvesting of the year's produce and the storing of some of it for use in winter. If you are just starting out in gardening, then get some produce from a friend or buy it in. Or, of course, if you are not too impatient you can wait for your own produce next autumn. The harvest is broadly in three categories, fruit, herbs and vegetables, and root crops (so called) and each needs different attention.

Harvest Festivals

In most Christian Churches in Western Europe and North America, a Sunday towards the end of September is chosen for the harvest festival, to which people bring examples of their produce. The festival is a thanksgiving to God for the bounty the earth provides. It is the same as Thanksgiving Day in the USA on the last Thursday in November; the celebration of the first harvest that the Pilgrim Fathers secured from their new home.

The theme is that we are stewards of the land and should both strive to gain from it and aim to leave it in as good, or even better, condition than we received it. This emphasises sustainability and ensures a continuing harvest in years to come. In earlier times, people made a Mother Earth figure or goddess, often from sheaves or stalks (the 'corn dolly'), again emphasising the stewardship of the land presided over by a deity.

Today in our largely urban and secular society, the origins of such festivals are all but forgotten and the occasion treated simply as a holiday. But it is good to remember our origins; how securing a harvest was a matter of life or death and, when it was safe, a cause for celebration. It may not be a matter of life and death in developed countries these days (supermarkets have seasonal produce all year round), but harvest can still be a cause for celebration within the family. It reminds both children and adults that we are not owners but stewards of the earth, that we should share with others what we produce. It gives a sense of thankfulness for the privilege of growing flowers, herbs and food.

Storing Fruit

Fruit is best eaten fresh from the garden. It tastes better and the freshness is a delight. We sometimes forget that the fruit and vegetables we buy from the supermarket may have come half-way around the world, having been picked many weeks before. In the UK the fruits of autumn are apples, pears, plums, damsons and the berries of rowan and elder, and rose hips.

If you are lucky enough to have access to an apple tree you can help with the apple harvest. You need to show children the gentle, twisting way with which to take the apple from the branch, making sure to keep the little stalk on the apple. If you do not it will keep less well. Late-ripening apples will keep best but they need a cool, frost-free, dark and dry shed or cupboard. You may have heard Bob Flowerdew on *Gardener's Question Time* on the radio extolling the virtues of old refrigerators for storing apples. You just need to make a little hole for ventilation. A problem in storing apples is that they tend to dehydrate, thus shrinking and becoming less palatable. Wrapping each apple in grease-proof paper helps.

Pointing to a fir tree you can ask 'Is this an apple tree?' 'No.' 'A holly?' 'No.' and so on until you reach a real apple tree. The relief is tremendous. The children can choose their apple to pluck and the small children have to be lifted up. They love the following poem.

Here stands a good apple tree.	*(stand upright)*
Stand firm at root.	*(stamp both feet)*
Bear well at top.	*(arms high)*
Every little twig	
Bear an apple big.	*(make apple shape with hands)*
Every little bough	
Bear an apple now.	*(both hands encouraging the tree to bear fruit)*
Hats full, caps full	
Hullo, folks, hullo.	

Anon

Bottling

Another way in which to keep surplus fruit for later is to cook it in the form of jams, jellies and by bottling. Jams and jellies are dealt with under the section 'Summer Harvest' (p.93). Bottling, unlike jam-making, does not require lots of sugar as a preservative. The principle underlying bottling is to destroy the germs by heat and also to prevent others from entering. You achieve this by sterilising the fruit in the jar and making a perfect seal. Probably the best jars are Kilner jars but any will do provided the lid will screw down tightly and make a good seal. Choose only the best fruit; that which is ripe but not over-ripe and without bruising.

To Bottle Fruit

Select and prepare the fruit (plums, damsons, cherries and so on) and then pack it tightly into clean jars. Top up to overflowing with cold water and screw on the tops loosely. Place the jars in a pan large enough to allow the jars to be immersed in water but not touching. Bring the water to simmering point and simmer for 10-15 minutes. Remove the jars using a pair of tongs and place on a wooden board. Screw the tops down tightly using cloths to hold the hot jar and top.

Something to Eat Now

We have been talking about preserving for the future. But the children will want something to eat, now. So, here is a simple recipe for:

Apple Fritters

Make a fritter batter of 113g self-raising flour, $1/4$ tsp salt, 2 eggs, 75ml milk, 14g butter, $1/4$ tsp lemon juice and 2 tsp brown sugar. Sieve the flour and salt into a bowl and place to one side. In another bowl, beat the eggs until fluffy. Add milk, butter, lemon juice and brown sugar and stir in. Add the flour and salt to the mixture and beat until smooth. Take 3 medium apples and peel, core and slice into rings. Heat enough oil (sunflower oil is good) to cover an apple ring. The oil is at the correct temperature when a drop of batter immediately rises to the surface and begins to brown. Dip each apple ring into the batter making sure it is thoroughly coated and slide into the hot fat. Fry until it is puffed up and golden brown. Drain on absorbent paper and keep warm. Serve dusted with caster sugar.

And here is an easy recipe for:

Baked Apples
Take several big apples and cut them in half at right angles to the core. Hollow out the core and fill with a mixture of raisins, chopped nuts, butter, a touch of cinnamon and brown sugar. Place on a greased baking tray in the oven at 150°C. They should be ready in 20 minutes. Test for softness with a skewer. They are delicious with ice cream on top.

Syrups and Jellies from Berries and Hips
Jelly (as distinct from a dessert jelly) is made in exactly the same way as jam (see p.94), except that after you have boiled up the fruit you strain the mixture through muslin to get rid of seeds and skins. Then with the clear liquid you proceed as for jam.

Fraser collecting rosehips

Rowan Jelly

The berries should be red and ripe in late August and September. Take all the stems off the berries and wash the fruit. Place in a pan and just cover the berries with water. Bring to the boil and continue until the berries have broken down. Allow to cool. Strain through muslin. Boil the resulting liquid. Take off the heat and add the sugar (0.45kg [1lb] of sugar to the same quantity of fruit), stirring until dissolved. Bring back to the boil and boil rapidly until the test for setting is satisfied (a little on a saucer and allow to cool; when the jelly is ready it will form a skin and flow less easily). Pour into warm sterilised jars and seal. Rowan jelly is a good and cheaper alternative to cranberry sauce with red meat.

Rose hips and elderberries can be made into a lovely syrup. Proceed as for rowan jelly but simply take the sugar-berry mixture back to the boil for a short time before pouring into warm sterilised bottles. The resulting syrup is diluted to taste with water or carbonated (fizzy) water.

Storing Vegetables and Herbs

Vegetables and herbs, like fruit, are best eaten fresh from the garden and some, like cabbage, brussel sprouts, broccoli and kale, can be left in the ground all winter and cropped as needed. In snowy weather you may have to protect them from woodpigeons and pheasants. You may also combine fruits and vegetables to make chutneys.

Herbs can be dried by hanging them in small bunches in the kitchen or in a dry shed but not in direct sunlight. Herbs freeze well and, of course, best of all they can be eaten fresh in salads.

Vegetables can be made into chutneys and pickles. This is similar to making jam except that sugar, as a preservative, is partly replaced by vinegar.

Vegetables such as onions, courgettes can be combined with tomatoes, apples and raisins to make chutneys. Here is a simple recipe:

Apple Chutney

The ingredients are: 2.6kg cooking apples, 0.45kg onions, 1 tsp ground ginger, 1 tsp salt, 1 tsp pickling spices, 0.68kg brown sugar and 0.8 litres balsamic vinegar. Peel and core the apples and peel the onions. Chop finely. Tie the spice in a piece of muslin. Put all the ingredients except the sugar and vinegar into a saucepan. Add enough vinegar to stop the ingredients from sticking to the pan and simmer gently for 1-2 hours, stirring occasionally. Add the vinegar and sugar and cook until the chutney is the consistency of jam. Pour into warm, clean jars and seal. Keep some weeks before use.

Storing Root Crops

Root crops such as carrots, parsnips, potatoes, turnips can all be very successfully stored throughout the winter. Turnips and swedes can be left in the ground and, in fact, benefit from exposure to frost. Onions and garlic are stored by hanging them up in bunches like herbs in a shed or in the kitchen.

Hanging onions up to dry

Broadly speaking, potatoes come in three main sorts: early, late early or early maincrop and maincrop. The early varieties are best used with the children (if you have to choose) because they give a crop soon and by planting inside in pots you can have delicious new potatoes at almost any time you wish. Depending on where you live, even outside planting will still give a meal in early summer. And new potatoes are delicious with a little butter and some chopped mint. Two good early varieties are Duke of York and Rocket. For a comprehensive list of potato varieties and their attributes see HDRA in 'References', p.135.

Early potatoes are not great croppers and so you will probably eat them all quite quickly. It is best to buy in certified early 'seed' potatoes each year to avoid the build-up of disease. However, if you want to save money you should select some potato plants, cut off the stems and

Olivia harvesting potatoes

leave the tubers in the ground for one-two weeks. The skins will toughen and the tubers will keep better.

Maincrop potatoes will not be ready until October. It is best to dig them up in dry weather and let them dry off for a few hours on plastic sheets before storing them.

Sort out the potatoes you have harvested: earlies into eating and 'seed' for planting; maincrop into medium tubers for planting, small and damaged for immediate eating and, if you have enough, some for storage; and also 'funny shapes' which can be used to make gnomes and birds and what you will. Two potato varieties which are knobbly are Pink Fir and Ratte (and they are good to eat too).

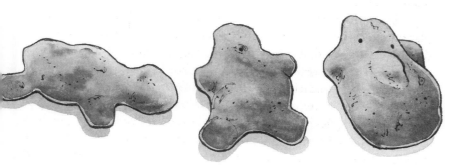

The obvious next step is a potato cooking session. If the children have sprouted them, planted and looked after them, harvested them, and now cook and eat them, it makes a beautifully complete whole.

If you have more than you need for the immediate future you can store them. Farmers make a 'clamp' to store root crops (potatoes, carrots, turnips). A clamp is a long conical heap of the crop, covered first with a thick layer of straw and then with a layer of earth, patted down flat with a spade. Gardeners rarely have enough of a crop to put it in a clamp but they can do something like it by storing small-scale in boxes lined with straw or paper, one layer deep, and set in a cool, frost-free shed in the dark. Check regularly for diseased individuals and remove them as they will contaminate the others.

Weeding and Mulching

Weeding is an important part of autumn preparation. If you are breaking in new ground you will have to persevere but, having cleared the ground, subsequent weeding will be quite an easy job. If you have the usual weeds of neglected ground such as thistles, nettles, couch grass, dock, rose bay willow herb (fireweed) and ground elder, you will have to dig deeply in order to get every last bit of root out. Even a piece half an inch long will grow again; that is why these tough weeds are so successful. But sometimes they tell the gardener something. For example, nettles in profusion usually means that the site is fertile. You see beds of nettles around derelict houses in the country where the midden or a well-worked garden used to be.

Once you have got rid of the established weeds, weed clearance is done by hoeing – a pleasant task provided it is done regularly. The green leaves that are cut off by the hoe can be left on the ground or raked around the base of established plants. Hoeing on a dry, hot, sunny day further ensures that weeds actually die. If the weeds are seeding, then probably you have not hoed often enough. Lift the seeding weeds, put them in the refuse bin (not in the composter as the seeds may not be destroyed there) and vow to hoe more often in future.

A **mulch** is a surface dressing of any organic or inorganic material which reduces the loss of moisture from the soil, suppresses weeds and keeps roots warm in winter and cool in summer. When made of compost and manure the mulch also feeds plants and improves the soil.

Mulches can be made from many materials. The most commonly used are garden compost, rotted horse or cow manure (often mixed with straw), bark chippings, black polythene, and, on plants in pots, gravel. Sawdust, wood-shavings and wood-chips are best not used around plants as they take a very long time to break down and initially take nitrogen from the soil to the detriment of the growing plant. Sawdust, wood-shavings and wood chips are best used on paths where they smother weeds and locally make the soil less fertile. The mineral content of wood ash varies greatly depending on the type of wood it comes from. Generally speaking, it is rich in potash and calcium, with much smaller amounts of phosphorus. The danger in using too much wood ash is that the concentration of potassium can reach a level at which it interferes with the soil's magnesium content by making it more soluble, so that it washes away; and also with trace elements such as boron and manganese. The presence of too much potassium (apple prunings are particularly rich in potassium) causes problems on heavy clay soils by making them even stickier. So use wood ash sparingly. Apply it to the soil immediately around crops, especially fruit, and rake it in.

Locally, other organic materials may be available such as seaweed, straw, spent mushroom compost and spent brewery waste.

Garden compost is precious stuff (all the more if you have made it yourself). It is therefore best saved for the growing season. Manure, even if not well rotted, can be spread over the ground in autumn; earthworms will pull it in over the winter. The soil structure, water retention properties and fertility of the soil will be increased.

Garden Tools for Children

Adult spades, hoes and rakes are too big and heavy for small children to use. You can cut down a hoe or rake; but kits of small tools are available with short extension pieces which make them entirely suitable.

CHAPTER 3

Winter

Feeding Birds in Winter

The North Wind doth blow and we shall have snow,
And what will the Robin do then, poor thing?
He'll fly to the barn and keep himself warm,
And put his head under his wing, poor thing.

'The North Wind shall blow and we shall have snow.'

The North Wind doth blow and we shall have snow,
And what shall the Swallow do then, poor thing?
Oh, did you not know, he's gone long ago,
To a country much warmer than ours, poor thing.

Anon

The   North Wind doth   blo - w   and   we shall have   sn - ow, And

what   will   the   Rob – in   do   then,   poor   thing?   He'll

fly   to   the   ba – rn   and   keep him – self   wa – rm, And

put   his   head   un – der   his   wing,   poor   thing.

Many birds leave the northern countries in winter because there is not enough food for them there. They often fly thousands of miles to spend our winter in Africa; examples are warblers, flycatchers and swallows. However, there are many kinds of birds which stick out our winter. Some winters are mild and the birds have a fairly easy time; more usually food is in short supply partly because it gets used up and partly

Robin

because ice and snow makes it difficult to find. You can help garden birds by feeding them; this helps them survive the winter and you have the pleasure of watching your bird table. An extra bonus is that you keep the birds in and around your garden so that in spring they can eat insects that you don't want.

The Bird Bell

Now is the time to use the seeds set aside in autumn together with raisins, crumbs, pea-nut butter and suet (vegetarian suet is available). If you were not able to collect enough seed earlier, you can buy large packets of mixed seed cheaply at pet shops and garden centres. You will also need a small plant pot for each child (5-7.5cm [2-3"] diameter). Clay pots are better than plastic because they grip the mixture and, being heavier, hang better. Plastic will do if you score the inside so that it holds the mixture. Or you can use half a coconut shell, but then you will need to drill a small hole in the end. You will also need a button and a length of string, the button big enough to cover the hole in the pot.

Mix the ingredients together in a big pot and heat gently giving the children a chance to stir.

Stir until melted and then let it set slightly (otherwise it will flow out of the hole in the plant pot).

Tie the string to the button and thread the string through the hole in the pot so that the button lies inside.

Pour the mixture into the pots and allow to set. Do this on a tray to contain spillage. The mixture sets quickly and the children will be able to hang their bird bell at the end of the morning. They can hang it from a branch in the garden or from a bracket outside the window. Hang it in a sheltered place and out of reach or predatory cats.

You may wonder how on earth a blue tit or great tit can possibly find the food upside down in a pot! But they can and do simply because they are constantly exploring every bit of their home ground, just like small children. The bell gives food to tits but keeps the larger birds away.

Here is a song to go with the bird bell:

Feed the birds in winter-time,
Help them find enough to eat,
Peanut butter, seeds and crumbs,
And suet for a special treat.

B. Lockie

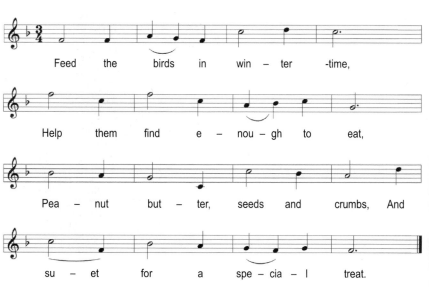

Other Ways to Feed Birds

You can string peanuts in their shells and hang them from a branch. This allows tits and also finches to feed. The finches have to balance a bit so that it is not made too easy for them. You can buy fat balls from pet shops and garden centres. The fat comes in a mesh bag which is hung up as before, and birds peck at the fat through the mesh. There are dispensers for seeds and nuts which have suckers; when the suckers are wetted and pressed against a window pane, they hold tightly. Tits, finches, even a woodpecker, will all visit these dispensers. How many different kinds of birds come to the food you put out?

A bird table is simply a flat ledge on which you can put all sorts of kitchen scraps. Because it is more accessible, it will be a free-for-all with blackbirds and starlings and even squirrels joining in. The table can stand free nailed to a post, or it can be hung on the wall of your house or as an extension to a window sill. It helps if the table has a low ledge on three sides to stop food from being kicked overboard. The fourth side is left open to allow easy cleaning. A roof keeps the worst of the weather off the food but it is not essential as the food is gobbled up in cold weather. Of course, you can buy a bird table in a garden centre; some are quite elaborate but I doubt if the birds appreciate this. Siting the table is important and there are three main considerations: first, put the table out in the open where cats cannot sneak up on the feeding birds; second, shelter it from wind; and third, put it where you can see and enjoy it.

At the end of the growing season many clumps of perennials die back and the temptation is to tidy everything up and dispose of the dead stems. Leave doing this as long as you can, at least in a part of the garden. The dead clumps give shelter and food for birds; and, if the stems are hollow, they provide a good winter shelter for ladybirds and lacewings. Indeed, you can gather dead hollow stems, tie them together in bunches, and hang them in a quiet part of the garden (see also p.49).

Lastly, give the birds water in freezing weather. They need water together with food and, when all is ice, replenish the water regularly. You can stop it from freezing by adding a little glycerine (from chemists), or a pinch of salt.

Making Nest Boxes

Most suburban gardens and young woodland have few, if any, natural holes for hole-nesting birds. So if we want to keep tits and robins in and around the garden all the year round, we have to provide not just food but also places for them to nest and rear young and even to sleep in very cold weather in winter.

Modern houses and out-buildings usually have no holes for bats to gain entrance to attics to roost, hibernate and breed. You can help them by putting up suitable boxes.

Bumblebees are useful in the garden for pollinating fruit blossom and flowers. They nest in banks and in holes in the ground. A suitable box is safer for them and you can put a glass panel in and see what is going on in the bumble bee world.

Lacewings and ladybirds are beneficial insects, both of which eat aphids (green-fly, black-fly). You can help them by providing hollow-stemmed plants for them to over-winter in.

Making nest boxes does not require great skill as a carpenter. Even so, a lot of the work is probably too difficult for young children. However, there are many aspects that a child can help with provided there is a guiding adult hand; and, of course, children like to be involved. Most birds begin seriously to investigate boxes by February so try to have your box up by then.

You will know if the bird box is in use by seeing the birds flying back and forth first with nesting material, then, when the young are small leaving with little bags of droppings (the dirty nappies) and bringing back food for hungry young (tits may have 8-12 young at a time). Once there are young, you can look in and see how many there are. If they are well-feathered, close the lid and leave them alone; otherwise they may take fright and leave the nest too early.

You will know if bats are living in your box because there will be a little heap of droppings on the ground under the box. And, at dusk in summer, you may see the bats leaving to hunt for insects. Don't disturb the box in winter as the bats will be hibernating.

Basic Nest Box for Hole-nesting Birds

Use a rough-sawn plank about 20mm ($^3/_4$″) thick and about 150mm (6″) wide. Mark off the sizes as shown in the diagram. The front will need a hole the diameter of which depends on the kind of bird you wish to attract. Sizes for common species are given in the table. Blue tits will get into a hole made for a great tit but the larger bird obviously cannot squeeze through the hole intended for a blue tit.

25mm (1″) for blue tit
28mm (1 $^1/_8$″) for great tit
32mm (1 $^1/_4$″) for house sparrow and nuthatch
45mm (1 $^3/_4$″) for starling
50mm (2″) for great spotted woodpecker

Starlings and woodpeckers will need more room than is offered in the basic box and increased sizes for them are shown in brackets beside the diagram for sawing. Woodpeckers excavate their nest cavities in dead trees, so fill up the box with sawdust or wood chips; the woodpeckers expect to do the excavating and we provide them with an easy means to do so.

You should drill some holes in the base for drainage. Assemble with galvanised nails or screws; if screws you will need to pre-drill say, the back, in order to screw this to the sides. When hammering nails or driving screws, put the box parts on a firm surface that you can push against. A piece of tough plastic acts both as a hinge for the lid and as seal to stop water from leaking into the box.

Do not fix a perch at the entrance hole to these boxes as it makes it easier for other birds to interfere with eggs and young.

Step-by-step Assembly

1.   Saw plank as diagram.

2.   Draw a line on the back piece 50mm (2″) from the end.

3.   Set sides against back and align the sides with the edge of the back and the line you have drawn; nail through back into the sides.

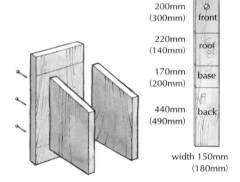

depth 20mm

250mm (300mm) — side

200mm (250mm) — side

200mm (300mm) — front

220mm (140mm) — roof

170mm (200mm) — base

440mm (490mm) — back

width 150mm (180mm)

4.   Align the bottom of the front with the bottom of the sides and nail from the front.

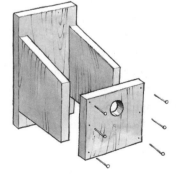

5. Place the bottom over the ends of sides and front and nail. Trim off the top of the front so that the lid can fit closely along its length.

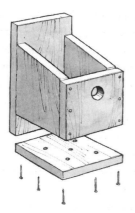

6. Secure the lid
    a) with a plastic hinge and
    b) by a screw on each side of the lid and a screw below each of these in the side. You can hold the lid tightly shut with wire between the screws.

7. Fasten firmly to a tree or wall and slightly tilted forward to keep rain out. For the tree, use nylon cord or wire stapled to the box and tied tightly to the tree. If you use wire, put it in a piece of hosepipe to protect the bark. If on a wall, use dowels and screws.

Boxes for tits, sparrows and starlings should be sited 2m (6') to 4m (12') from the ground on a tree or wall. A woodpecker box should be at least 5m (16') from the ground. Face the box north-east to avoid direct sunshine, and face away from the prevailing wind. Be sure that the birds have a clear flight path to the entrance.

Nest Box for Robins and Flycatchers

Both these kinds of birds need a box very similar to that already described except that instead of an entrance hole they prefer a large open front. So, cut the wood as before. Then cut the front in half and use one half for the front. Boxes for robins and flycatchers need to be sited lower than the others mentioned and, above all, be well hidden in vegetation. A good place would be 1-2m (3-6') up a wall and behind a shrub.

Boxes for Bats

Three kinds of bat are widespread in Britain; the pipistrelle (the smallest), the long-eared, and Daubenton's bat. All are gregarious in summer and autumn but in winter, while the pipistrelle hibernates in large colonies, often squeezing into a small space, the other two hibernate in small groups or singly.

Bats will readily use nest boxes if they are placed under the eaves of a building or high in a tree (say, 5-7m [15-20']). We can use exactly the same design of box as for hole-nesting birds except:

1. Omit the hole in the front;
2. Saw 20mm ($^3/_4$") off the base of the box; this allows you to leave a gap between the rear of the base and the back. Bats enter the box through this gap from below;
3. Before assembly, if you have used smooth wood, saw shallow grooves across the inside of the nest box parts, including the roof, to give bats something to cling to when they are roosting. Make parallel saw-marks below the entrance also. This is to make it easier for the bats to climb in. If you have used rough-sawn wood, the surface will probably be entirely suitable for bats to cling to.

Box for Bumblebees

Bumblebees nest in holes in banks, in mouse nests and even in the nest boxes put up for birds. So we can modify our basic nest box to suit the bees.

First, omit the normal entrance hole at the front and instead drill a hole of 30mm (1 $^1/_4$″) diameter near the bottom of the front. Into this is pushed, as a tight fit, a length of plastic pipe. This tube is the entrance hole for the bees. Cut off the bottom two inches of the back of the box so that the box stands without support.

The box is best half-buried in the ground, south-facing under a hedge or against an old wall with vegetation around. Dig a hole larger and deeper than the box and line the bottom with stones to give good drainage. Place the box in the hole, lead the tube out and to the surface about 50cm (20″) away from the box. Fill the hole with stones level with the surrounding ground. The tube should stick out about 50mm (2″) from the surface.

Make a ball of dry, fine grasses and dry moss about 75-100mm (3-4") and place it inside the box. Tie down the lid tightly. You could add a refinement by putting a glass panel under the wooden lid held, with 'bluetack' or similar. You will then be able to look inside without disturbing the bees.

Bumblebees will be looking for homes in early May when the queen will be prospecting; and, when she has decided, she will familiarise herself with the surrounding area. Later, you will see worker bees arriving with food. Bumblebees can sting but are generally pretty placid.

Shelters for Lacewings and Ladybirds
The hollow stems of hogweed, fennel, angelica and other umbellifers are an ideal hibernating place for many insects including lacewings and ladybirds.

Because winter storms of snow and rain smash these stems down, we can help these insects by gathering up some of the hollow dried stems, tying them in bunches and hanging them in a sheltered

Lacewing

part of the garden. Hang them about waist high on a shed, on the leeward side of a fence, or on a shrub. You can give them even greater protection by using the basic nest box. Omit the front. Cut the hollow stems into 150mm lengths (6"), tie lightly into bundles and stack them, holes outwards to fill the box. Keep them in place with some nylon netting held with drawing pins.

Ladybirds on leaf

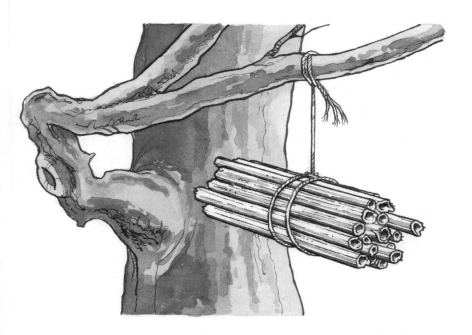

Shelters for lacewings and ladybirds

St. Martin's

This is a lantern festival held on 11th November. Children can make small paper or turnip lanterns and process round the garden, singing. It can be magical to see the wonder on a young child's face as he carries his little light into the darkness. This festival is based on the following story:

The Story of St. Martin

Once upon a time there was a nobleman who, while travelling home late one night, saw a beggar sheltering under an archway. The beggar was shivering with cold as he had only meagre rags to cover him. The nobleman, called Martin, felt such compassion for the beggar that he took his sword, cut his cloak in two, and gave him half of it. That night he had a dream in which angels showed him the cloak with a cross upon it. In a flash he realised he was being called to care for needy people. In doing so, he became the patron saint of beggars.

Advent

Advent is the period extending through the four Sundays before Christmas. In the Christian tradition we light a candle every Sunday until all four candles are lit on the last Sunday, heralding the birth of Christ, a light in the world.

The four candles can be set on a wreath made from fir branches and tied with red ribbons; or the wreath may be hung on the front door of the house. You can also, of course, have an Advent calendar, the children taking turns to open a door each day of Advent until 25th December, when the last door reveals the Christ child in a manger.

The Advent Garden
Advent is a well-known period in the Christian calendar, but the Advent garden is less well-known. It was probably first devised by Karl König, and is part of the gradually increasing use of candles through the autumn, first at Michaelmas and then at St. Martin's with lanterns, culminating in the great festival of Christmas, symbol of light in darkness.

For both children and adults the Advent garden can be a moving experience. In a room which can subsequently be darkened, the adults prepare a big spiral made of moss and evergreen branches, leaving a path wide enough to walk to the middle. Here at the centre there is a hillock of moss on top of which is placed a large fat candle (the mother candle). On the moss of the spiral you can put decorations of, say, crystals, berries and pine cones. On a little table at the entrance to the room are rosy red apples on a tray, each with a beeswax candle firmly fixed in it, one for each child (and a few spares for unexpected visitors).

I find it difficult to decide whether to make the garden a complete surprise, not even glimpsed beforehand, or to have children join in the preparation as part of their gardening programme. I tend to compromise and let the older children prepare for the younger ones. It is certainly great to have a few pairs of energetic hands to carry moss and branches. By helping prepare it, the Advent garden becomes more meaningful for the older children; and the younger ones still have their surprise.

The children enter an almost darkened room with perhaps a few candles on high shelves to give a little light so that they can find their way and so that it is not frighteningly dark. The children find seats

around the walls of the room. Then, very, very softly, a lyre* or similar
instrument begins to play. This need not be a recognisable tune; soft
chords are preferable in order to create the right mood. The teacher or

---

*   A simple stringed instrument, usually tuned to a pentatonic scale.

parent walks slowly into the centre of the spiral and lights the mother candle speaking the following verse:

The gift of light I thankfully take,
But not to keep it just for my sake:
The more we give light the one to the other,
The more shall we be like sister and brother.

Anon

The adult then moves back to his or her place. The music continues while the teacher or parent beckons to the eldest child who comes forward and receives his apple with candle. The child goes into the spiral, right up to the mother candle, lights his candle and then places the apple with candle anywhere on the spiral. This continues child after child, and the room gradually fills with light.

When all the candles have been planted, the eldest child returns to the spiral, collects his apple and candle, blows the candle out and returns to his place taking apple and candle with him. This continues until all the children have retrieved their apple and candle. Then the adult goes to the centre and extinguishes the mother candle. The children can use their candle, under supervision, during Advent at home and in the kindergarten renewing the candle as necessary.

The Advent garden must be under constant supervision. There is little danger of fire especially as the moss is damp. However, just to be sure, have a fire blanket and an extinguisher or water to hand.

Celebrating a festival in this way, and the spiral form itself, goes deeply into young children. You will notice that they replay it often with each other, with dolls and with sisters, brothers and friends. It is better that they go quietly home after this experience and are allowed some 'space' to let their feelings consolidate – rather than be taken, for example, to a busy supermarket. There should be no other kindergarten activity either after the festival.

The Story of the Christmas Rose

A lovely story to tell the children is the following, of the little girl Beth and the Christmas Rose.

Once upon a time, there was a little girl called Beth who lived with her grandmother as both her parents had died. They lived in a forest in a small wooden house. They loved each other dearly and were very happy together.

One day each week they walked to the nearby village. They each carried a basket, Grandma the bigger and Beth the smaller. It was bitterly cold and Grandma said, 'This is just the sort of cold that comes before snow. I don't think it can be far away so we had better not linger in case we get caught in a snow-storm.' Well, that is just what happened. Because they lived in the forest and hardly ever met anyone, it was so nice to chat and hear all the news and to choose their shopping slowly and carefully. So they stayed longer in the village than they had meant to.

At last they set off home. By now the sky was very dark and heavy and it felt as though a great blanket would fall on top of them. Grandma and Beth walked as fast as they could but the old woman could not keep up with the young girl. 'Please Beth, not so fast,' she pleaded. The first snowflakes started to form, at first tiny then larger, until soon they came so thick and fast that, had they not known the forest so well, they might have lost their way.

Grandma started to cough and to fall behind. When Beth noticed it she walked back and took Grandma's basket and supported her with her arm. 'I can't go on,' sighed the old woman. 'Yes you can, we are almost there,' said Beth; and she went on talking to Grandma about the fire she would light (wasn't it all set and only needed a match?), the soup she would warm and how soft and cosy her bed would be. How long it seemed to the house although they must be quite near now. Grandma leaned more heavily on Beth's arm. She stopped every now and then to cough and to sigh and to Beth the two baskets were becoming unbearably heavy, not to mention Grandma leaning heavily on her.

'How I would like to play with the snow fairies,' thought Beth. When they at last arrived at the cottage, Beth saw to everything, to the fire, to hot soup for her Grandma after she had tucked her up in bed with a hot water bottle. Beth did not go out until Grandma was fast asleep. Then Beth went to the door and looked out. By now it was dark outside, but the thick covering of snow made everything look clean and beautiful. She thought of other children who were

'…and then tucked her up in bed with a hot water bottle'

free to go out and play in the snow. It was getting colder and colder. As she stood there, Beth could not help but cry a little and the salt tears fell on the snow and melted it.

Next day the sun shone and made everything look like fairyland. 'Go on' said Grandma 'I am better now thanks to you, dear child. The snow fairies are still there waiting for you to come out to play.' Beth wrapped up warmly and when she stepped out of the door where she had stood the night before feeling so sad, she saw something she had not noticed before. There at her feet had grown a plant right through the snow and on its branches hung a cluster of white flowers. She gently picked some and took them into Grandma. Grandma thanked Beth and smiled. 'There now, that is your reward from the fairies for looking after others before pleasing yourself.'

The flower was a Christmas Rose and it came back every Christmas after that.

Anon

Christmas roses (hellebores)

If you have children around you on Christmas Eve, it is an unforgettable experience to go into the darkness and listen with your ear against the bark of trees, to the sap beginning to rise slowly and so softly, until in spring it begins to flow.

CHAPTER 4

Spring

Winter into Spring

In recent years, it seems that autumn has tended to push into winter, and winter into spring. In Scotland the spring is so short that you find yourself suddenly in summer. Superimposed on this is the ocean-dependent climate of Britain which can vary from day to day. Although there are days in winter and early spring when you can sit outside in shirt-sleeves: more usually the weather is cold, dull, often with rain and frost or snow. And frost can continue at times into April and May and even early June. The consequence of this is that you must not rush to plant outside; instead, be patient and wait until the weather is more stable and the soil has warmed up. Get the children to test the warmth of the soil with the back of their hand and feel it improve over the weeks. It also means that you may have to delay planting out sprouted potatoes until all chance of frost has passed (or protect them). In Scotland you may have to wait until early June; in the south of England you may get away with it in early May. Obviously it is necessary for gardeners to know not only their climate but also local weather patterns.

The change from winter to spring starts long before it becomes obvious to the casual viewer. There are the signs of shoots pushing through the earth long before they form buds and later leaves and flowers. There is a subtle change in the light although the evening darkness still comes too early for our liking. If there are several days of sunshine, even if it is cold, the grass begins to look different and even to grow in sheltered places. Above all there are days in spring when the feeling in the air is of the whole of nature just bursting to grow.

Then we see the first daisies in the grass and, in the woods, the yellow celandine. If you look at trees at this time you will see different kinds of catkin; alders and willows have catkins on different trees and the male catkins are larger and sometimes more showy. First come the bright yellow willow catkins and then the alder. Later come those of hazel and birch. You can bring these catkins indoors and let them blossom. The yellow dust that will fall on the table is pollen. You could buy daffodils and put a few with the catkins to make a nice effect.

But the snowdrop is special. It comes before all the catkins. It is so brave, it blossoms in cold and rain and even in snow. And, as it is so special, here is a story about the snowdrop.

How the Snowdrop got its Colour

After Father God had created all the plants and flowers, He wanted to give them beautiful colours. So He gave the forget-me-not blue, the marigold orange, the iris a deeper blue, the roses pink, red, and yellow and so on until they were all done. The angels were very busy painting the flowers all the colours of the rainbow and when they were ready they looked beautiful. But

the angels forgot that while they were painting all the flowers of spring, summer and autumn, there was one little flower that had grown up and faded before any of the others had even appeared. It was the very first flower of the year, yes, the snowdrop.

When the snowdrop heard that all the other flowers had been given colours, it began to be sad that it had been missed out. 'Why me?' it sighed, 'I know that I am only little but I too would like to have a colour. I know, I'll ask the other flowers to give me a little of theirs. They are sure to agree.' So up the snowdrop went to a yellow tulip. 'Please Mr. Tulip, could you share some of your yellow with me as I haven't got any colour?' Said the tulip: ' What? I need it all for myself. When I flower in spring there usually isn't much sun yet and I have to shine as hard as I can.' The snowdrop understood and thanked the tulip nicely.

Next it saw a forget-me-not: 'Please Miss Forget-me-not, can you give me some of your beautiful blue because they have left me out?' The forget-me-not answered, 'Blue, blue, not for you; blue's for me, for me, you see'. And on and on it went saying the same words over and over again. The marigold was next. 'Please Mrs. Marigold, may I have some of your cheerful orange; I only need a little. You see, they have forgotten me'. 'Some of my beautiful bright sunny orange? No fear; it wouldn't suit you at all; it only suits me. Try another flower'. And so saying she turned her back on the poor snowdrop.

They all seemed to be the same; they didn't want to share. Should the snowdrop just stop now and try to be content with no colour? No, it would

Said the forget-me-not:
'Blue, blue, not for you,
blue's for me, for me, you see.'

'...the haughty rose
gave the snowdrop
a nasty prick'

have one more go. It approached a lovely red rose with the same request. But the snowdrop had hardly finished speaking when the haughty rose gave the snowdrop a nasty prick with its thorns. 'Never! It's all mine. It was given to me and it stays with me.'

The snowdrop was not only sad, it was a little offended. Never was it going to ask for a favour again. In its sorrow it bent its head right down. And then it started to snow. When the snow saw the sad little plant, it whispered 'What is happening here and why are you so bent down?' The snowdrop sighed and told the snow that all the plants had colours and that the angels had run out of colours and forgotten the snowdrop. And so it was left all green like grass and leaves. How it longed for a colour of its very own. 'That is easy' said the snow, 'I'll give you some of mine. I have plenty to share.' So the snow started to cover the snowdrop with a white, pure and clean, until it looked beautiful. But you know, if you look carefully at the snowdrop flower, you will see a few bits of green that the snow did not quite cover up. From that day onwards, the snowdrop and the snow were very good friends; that is why they always come together. 'I will not harm you with my cold,' promised the snow.

Anon

People love the snowdrop as it is the very first flower in spring and gives them hope after the dark days of winter.

Candlemas

After the New Year celebrations, 2nd February is the first festival of the year. Candlemas is not generally known or celebrated but, in the olden days and sometimes continuing to the present day, this was the time when farmers and owners of land walked around the boundary of their property. I knew of one small landowner who, until his death around 1970, dressed up in his best clothes and, with a top hat, 'walked the Marches'. It is also the time that snowdrops appear. In some parts they are called Candlemas Bells.

We can celebrate this day by lighting up the first candles of the year. But where do candles come from? Well, nowadays they are made in factories although there are still people who make a living out of candle making. If they can do it, so can you! Here is a step-by-step means to make your own candles:

1. Take two deep tins and fill them with candle ends collected over the last year (or buy candle wax in bulk from a crafts shop). Heat one tin over a medium flame. The other tin goes on the heat while candle-dipping is in progress.

2. Prepare the candle wicks which you can make from lengths of white cotton string. Attach a small weight to one end so that the wick hangs vertically (a washer will do). Cover the floor around the work table with newspapers to catch drips.

3. When the wax is properly melted (but not smoking!), place the tin on a table where the children can reach it and let the children dip the weighted wicks into the wax so that the weight reaches the bottom of the tin.

4. Withdraw the wick and hold for a moment to let the wax congeal. Then walk round the table to let the wax harden before the next dip. If it is not hard enough the wax at the next dip will simply slide off. So, how do you know when the wax is hard? Put your finger on the wax; it should feel cool and you should not leave a finger mark on the wax.

5. Dip again and repeat until the candle is fat enough.

6. If the wax on the table begins to congeal, then swap it with the tin now heating.

The story of the snowdrop reminds us of our crocuses which are waiting in the dark cupboard. They are ready to be taken out into the light now and soon the bud will begin to show. This is the moment when child can take it home or take it to his own room and continue to care for it. Remind children and parents to bring the pot and bulb back after flowering so that so that it can be planted outdoors next autumn.

Watering

Watering is one of the gardener's most important activities. It is easy to spray or pour water on but much more difficult to get the amount just right. Plants can suffer from too much and too little water. It is not good practice to give a bit extra. The water you do put on can be conserved by applying a mulch to the soil around the plant (see p.34).

In open ground, where water can drain away, the amount you put on is not so critical. You do, however, want the water to go where it will most benefit the plant and that is the root system. It is better to give smaller amounts often rather than a deluge seldom. You can check if your watering has got to the roots by digging down to one side of the plant to see if the water has reached the level of the roots.

Water is essential for all plants but some need larger than usual amounts at certain times; treat them well and they will flourish. For example, potatoes need extra water at the time when the tubers are beginning to grow, which is when the potatoes are in flower. In the same way, beans and peas in flower need extra water to produce full pods.

Lettuces and leaf crops need to be well-watered throughout their season. On the other hand, flowering plants sometimes need a little shock to start flowering: by reducing water you can persuade them to flower. If you keep giving lots of water, they will carry on merrily making leaves!

Seedlings and more mature plants need a good soaking immediately after planting out from pots to open ground. The aim is to wash fine soil down to the roots so that they can have close contact; this hurries the establishment of the plant in its new home. After this first soak, go on to normal watering regularly.

Cuttings need to be kept moist (see p.101). Drying out, even if followed by a soaking, usually means the death of the cutting. It is

usual, when preparing a cutting, to reduce the number of leaves so that the cutting does not give off too much water. It helps against dehydration to cover the cutting and pot with a plastic bag.

Plants in pots, particularly those inside but also pots against sheltering walls, depend on you for all their water. So you must give enough to moisten all the compost in the pot every day in summer but less as the plants cease to grow in autumn and winter.

Rain Water versus Tap Water

Tap water is treated to prevent the spread of disease. The most common addition is chlorine, a substance found in bleach. Many plants do not take kindly to a daily dose of chlorine, so if you can arrange for water to run off your roof or off a corrugated iron or plastic sheet into a container, this is better than tap water. Some industrial areas still pollute the air and the rain that falls through it. Much of the UK is much cleaner than it used to be, but if you have doubts ask your local Environmental Protection Agency office.

Sowing Seed and Sprouting Potatoes Inside

In early spring it is best to sow some seed inside so that it is sheltered and warm and germinates quickly. Then the plant can grow on until strong enough and the soil is warm enough for it to be planted out. By this means you extend the season.

Get out boxes and pots to sow lettuce, parsley and chives and any herbs you wish to put in the Communal Garden (see p.78). This is a good moment to mention the four elements EARTH, FIRE, WATER, and AIR, although not in these words, of course. For small children it is always best to express them in pictures, for instance with the 'Mother Earth' song on p. 25.

Broad beans now replace crocuses, which have gone home to be tended there.

Start by soaking the beans in water overnight and have a look at the black spot out of which the bean shoot will appear and which has to point upwards when you plant the bean.

Going through the ritual of stones in the bottom and soil from Mr. and Mrs. Mole is great because the children will say 'I know that already'.

Plant the beans 5cm (2") below the surface. Don't forget to bless the earth.

Now names on pots and occasional watering, and when the beans are established plants, they go home where the children will continue to look after them.

It is amazing (or perhaps not so amazing!) how many bean plants will have died or got lost when the time comes to bring them back to be planted outside. Many other things may claim the child's attention and the parents should gently remind the child that they should care for the plant. It will mean a lot to them when it later flowers and produces big pods. Of course the teacher or parent has spares ready to replace those lost – but don't advertise the fact beforehand.

A nice song for sowing:

A farmer once planted some little brown seeds, (repeat)
With a pit-a-pat here and a pit-a-pat there, (repeat)
He watered them often and pulled out the weeds, (repeat)
With a tug tug at this and a tug tug at that, (repeat)
The little seeds grew tall in the sun, (repeat)
With a push push up here and a push push up there, (repeat)
And a beautiful flower grew from every one, (repeat)
With a heigh-ho and diddle and we'll have such fun. (repeat)

Anon

1.   A –   far – mer once plan - ted some lit – tle brown seeds,
2.   He –   wat –ered them of - ten and pulled out the   weeds,
3.   The –   li – tt – le   se – eds grew tall in   the   sun,

1.   With a   pit – a – pat here   and a   pit – a – pat   there,
2.   With a   tug tug at this   and a   tug tug at   that,
3.   With a   push push up here   and a   push push up   there,

1.   With a   pit – a – pat here   and a   pit – a – pat   there,
2.   With a   tug tug at this   and a   tug tug at   that,
3.   With a   push push up here   and a   push push up   there,

4.   And a   beau – ti – ful   flo - wer grew from eve - ry   one,

4.   With a   heigh - ho and   did - dle and we'll ha – ve   such   fun,

4.   With a   heigh - ho and   did - dle and we'll ha – ve   such   fun.

Potatoes can be put on a window-sill to sprout. Put them in an egg carton with the eyes pointing upwards.

You are now doing the opposite of what you did to store potatoes. Then you kept them in a cool dry place to stop the eyes from sprouting and the skin from turning green (when they contain the poison solanine). Inside on a window-sill the potatoes will get light and warmth and the skin will tend to turn green (but it does not matter now). The eyes will begin to sprout. The idea is to produce strong green shoots before planting out. In this way the potatoes can start the business of growing before the weather allows these frost-sensitive plants to be put outside.

The Children's Garden

Much has been said about whether children should have their own plot or should share a garden. On the one hand, one always wants to introduce and encourage a social element and this is helped by sharing and tolerating others. At the same time it is difficult for the small child to understand this as they always want to have something of their very own. So, I suggest a combination of both ideas. The individual gardens are set in a circle like the petals of a buttercup. The circle, by its magical form, helps to hold the children together. The central plot forms the shared garden where the children cooperate. It might look like this.

In the middle, in the shared part, you could build a tepee of sticks on which to grow sweet peas or runner beans.

As spring progresses and the weather gets better, there is plenty to do in the garden. Whether you are a teacher or a parent, try to take one day of the week that comes to be known as 'gardening day'; the children will more easily remember the first day of the week. As always, looking forward to the event is half the pleasure. Nevertheless, the golden thread of nature continues thought the rest of the week, albeit to a lesser degree, if the teacher or parent introduces new flowers. The flowers have to be named, of course, and it is good fun to explore the local names of common wild flowers. Take the common daisy. Who would believe that it has between 30 and 40 local names. Here are some of them: Baby's Pet, Billy Button, Curl Doddy, Day's Eye, Innocent, Silver Pennies, White Frills and Twelve Disciples. What a wealth of material or making up short stories for small children (see Geoffrey Grigson's *The Englishman's Flora* in the bibliography).

As spring progresses we search for all the buds and flowers as they appear. Each morning we lay the flowers on a veil, perhaps colour by colour. One can hardly keep up with the speed of appearance of flowers and the veil that they are spread on gets bigger and bigger. Sometimes, in their enthusiasm, children will pick flowers that you don't want them to pick. But we must not be too hard on them: they will learn in time, especially if they are given a good example.

Now we have a lovely game. We arrange ourselves around a room in a circle and say the following verse:

On each branch of every tree,
Just as tight as tight can be,
Lots of leaves and buds we see,
Cuddling close together.

B. Lockie

On the last line we creep forward on our knees until we touch and, with lots of laughter, fall about and hug each other.

As soon as the soil is reasonably dry and a good day presents itself, you can go into the plot that will be the children's garden; and, in a long snake (depending on how many children you have) start treading the paths. First, mark out the individual plots that you have sketched on paper. If you have access to wood chips or similar, use these as markers and subsequently the little paths will be weed free. But if you have no wood chips, tramp the soil hard and that will do well enough. You can make up a little chant which always adds to the enjoyment.

Tramp, tramp here we go,
Making the paths between just so,
Not too wide and not too long,
Stamping with our tramping song.

B.Lockie

Planting Out

To a Friend Planting

Proceed, my friend, pursue thy healthful toil,
Dispose thy ground and meliorate thy soil,
Range thy young plants in walk or clumps or bow'rs,
Diffuse o'er sunny banks thy fragrant flow'rs,
And, while the new creation round thee springs,
Enjoy unchecked the guiltless bliss it brings.

John Scott, 1730-83

It is important to begin with planting not sowing. This sounds the wrong way round but it is for a very practical reason. The children cannot be expected to remember exactly where (even with markers) and in what shape they sowed their seeds. And so, you avoid planting on top of sowings and avoid disappointment.

You can start with wild flowers from the corners of your garden. The common plants I use are daisy, buttercup, dog violet and forget-me-not. The daisy and buttercup are recognised weeds (when they are in the wrong place). Both are lovely flowers and just think of the fun the children get out of: 'Do you like butter?' (Hold the flower under someone's chin and if there is a yellow reflection the answer is 'Yes'.)

The adult shows how to dig the first plant out. Make sure that all the roots are included together with as much soil as possible so that the plant is disturbed as little as possible. Now the children can try. The children can choose where to plant within their plot but it is necessary to guide them as the adult alone knows what else is going to be put in and what size it will grow to. I take one kind of plant each week in order to stretch the work out a bit.

Dig a hole with a trowel deep enough to accommodate all the roots without cramping them. Add some compost.

Place the plant in the hole. Water the roots. Fill the hole in bit by bit with layers of soil, gently pressing each layer down around the plant to keep the soil in contact with the roots.

Then water again. If there is no rain, you will have to water the plants every day until they are established.

You will know that they are established and happy when the flowers and leaves hold themselves up and are stiff and therefore full of water.

Strawberries can also be planted out. Follow the same procedure but, in addition, put dry straw around the plants to keep the ripening berries off the ground where they might rot. By keeping them off the ground you also deter slugs which demolish strawberries if given half a chance.

> Theocrastes gives us great Caution in Planting, to preserve the roots and especially the Earth adhering to the smallest Fibrils, which should by no means be shaken off as most of our Gardeners do. Not at all considering, that those tender Hairs are the very mouths and vehicles that suck in the Nutriment, and transfuse it into all parts of the Tree, and once perishing, the thicker and larger roots signify little but to support the stem.
>
> *John Evelyn, 1662*

All planting out follows pretty much the same procedure. So, now is the time to bring the broad beans back from home. Tears may have to be dried over beans that have been lost, or dried up or been grossly over-watered. But the ever-resourceful teacher or parent will have replacements up her sleeve. Often, the bean, having grown too tall in the warmth inside, needs a crutch to stop it from falling over. Use a thin cane stuck into the ground and tie the bean gently with wool. Or the bean can be given a haircut to make it less top-heavy. But this is something to be done only by an adult. It is simple: trim with scissors some of the side shoots but leave the leading shoot. After an initial shock the bean will recover quickly. So plant out your broad bean in your own garden in the way described above. The bean, of course will be in a pot. Gently tap and shake the pot while holding the stem of the bean. Be careful and gentle or the stem will break. The roots will come out of the pot with the soil or compost you have used wrapped around it. Keep it intact and place in the hole you have dug in the individual gardens, carefully fill up with soil, and water it in.

If the bean has produced so many roots that they have grown out of the bottom of the pot, you have two options: first, gently try to tease the roots through the holes of the pot – you will break some but others will remain intact. Second, if the bean (or any other plant) is in a plastic pot, carefully cut the pot with sharp scissors or pliers and extricate the roots from the dismembered pot.

Hardening Off

All planting out follows the same procedure except that, if your plants have been grown inside in warmth, it may be necessary to toughen them up before they go out into the real world. If you have a cold frame then put the plants in their pot inside it for a few days. If you don't have one, put them outside in a sheltered place and be prepared to bring them in again should there be a late frost or strong winds. This procedure is called 'hardening off'.

Planting Potatoes

When the potatoes are well-sprouted (that is, with sprouts about 3-4cm [1-1½″] long), we can plant them out. If the sprouts are much longer they will be easily broken off by accident. There will be several sprouts on each tuber. The number of sprouts that the tuber is allowed to retain is decided by the number and size of the tubers you want. Other things being equal, one sprout will mean a small number of large tubers, two sprouts medium-sized tubers and three or more will give many small potatoes. You get rid of unwanted sprouts by gently rubbing them off with a fore finger; they break off easily. In fact, watch out that those small fingers don't wipe all the sprouts away in their enthusiasm. Now dig a hole about 15cm (6″), deep (approximately the length of an adult hand) and place the potato in the bottom with the sprouts upwards. Gently fill the hole with soil but don't press the soil down too hard or the sprouts will be broken. Pull some soil around the spot to leave a little mound as a marker.

Once potatoes grow up and have a lot of leaf above the ground, they become susceptible to 'blight', which is a fungus. Blight is especially prevalent when the weather is warm, humid and still. The first signs are blackening of the leaves, spreading from the tips. If it is allowed to go on the haulms will wither but what is worse, after rain, the spores of the fungus will be washed into the ground where they will rot the potatoes. You can save the day by promptly spraying with Bordeaux Mixture (a copper sulphate solution, entirely natural, which you can buy in garden centres). If you have a really bad attack later in the season it is best to dig up the potatoes immediately, wash them well, and use them quickly rather than storing them. Destroy the haulms in some way and do not put them on the compost heap.

Sowing Outside

Before doing any sowing we must prepare the soil so that the particles are small and so that small seeds don't get lost in big clods of earth. It involves raking the soil, breaking up large bits and removing stones that come to the surface as you work. It is called producing a fine tilth. Heavy clay soils are rich in minerals but difficult to work. In wet weather they become sticky and adhere to everything: spades, boots, rakes and so on. They drain badly and during extended dry weather can set hard as concrete. During autumn it is therefore good to dig in copious amounts of compost together with sharp sand and grit. In spring, when the soil is not too wet, crumble it with a hand tool. It may take time but the resulting soil will be worth the effort.

As the ground warms up we can sow cress in the individual gardens. The good thing about cress is that it comes up very soon after sowing, perhaps in three days. Cress also gives the children a continuous crop. Cut it with scissors and it comes again. After the first harvest, show them how to use it on a sandwich with a little honey and a squeeze of lemon, or use it in a salad.

Sowing a row of fine seeds is a tricky business for small fingers. We can first practise sowing inside. Give the children a large sheet of paper. On this, draw in colour a simple figure or their initials. The teacher then demonstrates how to shake the seeds gently out of the packet onto the pattern on the paper so that they don't all pour out at once. Put the seeds back in the packet and let each child try. The others will be watching intently and learning.

Outside now, and choose a windless day.
Everyone gets a short stick as thick as your
finger. The teacher shows how to draw the
figure or initials in the soil making a
continuous shallow V (no more than
1¼cm (½") deep by dragging the point of
the stick along the soil.

Now water the V thoroughly.

The seeds are then sown in the V, covered
with Mother Earth and pressed down firmly
with your hand.

Later, once the first seeds have come up
and, if you want a succession of fresh salad greens, you can sow
repeatedly at intervals so that you have fresh salad crops until autumn
when you can think about sowing winter lettuce. (See section on slug
control p.87!) Successional sowing is successful with salad crops but you
could also sow broad beans and peas and herbs in the same way. This
extends the season and also may allow a surplus to be frozen or dried.

Sowing Beans

One for the mouse,
One for the crow,
One to rot,
and one to grow.

Anon

May Day

The first day of May is by tradition the beginning of summer even if summer comes earlier or later depending where you are in the country.

In Celtic countries, May Day is celebrated by the Beltane Festival in which a Beltane or May Queen, carrying a bouquet of May or hawthorn blossom, is escorted in procession to a nearby hill-top there to preside over a bonfire and singing and dancing. It is still celebrated today in Scotland, and in Edinburgh the procession climbs to the top of the Calton Hill in the centre of the city.

It is also a tradition to wash one's face in May dew, said to be good for the complexion. And I know of couples, about to be or just married, who have climbed to the top of a hill early on May Day to restate their marriage vows.

The specialness of the first of May lives on from very early times. Hawthorn blossom is characteristic of the month.

The Song of the May Fairy

My buds they cluster small and green;
The sunshine gaineth heat;
Soon shall the Hawthorn tree be clothed
As with a snowy sheet.

O magic sight, the hedge is white,
My scent is very sweet;
And lo, where I am come, indeed
The Spring and Summer meet.

Cicely Mary Barker

The Communal Garden

In between the fairly hectic planting and sowing, we have to think of the centre patch or communal garden. As mentioned earlier, a runner bean or sweet pea tepee, according to your local climate, makes a good centre piece. In the north, the summer is often not long enough or consistently warm enough for runner beans to give a decent crop but the red flowers, at least, will flourish. Sweet peas will do well almost anywhere and the more you pick them, the more flowers they will produce so that the children will be able to take small bouquets home.

For the tepee, use as many poles as you want divisions to plant herbs. I use seven poles about 2m long. Push them a little into the ground at regular intervals round the centre plot and tie them together at the top with wire or twine. Put compost on the area where the seeds or beans are going to be sown. If you plant runner beans, then follow the same procedure as you did for the broad bean (soaking overnight before sowing and making sure that they are the right way up). Sow sweet peas in the way described earlier in a V trench about 1¼cm (½") deep. Beans and sweet peas will climb all over the tepee.

You have already sown some herbs inside in pots so that they benefit from a little warmth when germinating. Once they are established plants they should be put outside in a sheltered place for a week or so to become stronger – the process called 'hardening off'. After that they can be planted out in the centre garden. Now that you have made a start, you can fill in gaps in the individual gardens with wild flowers. Always follow the same ritual: dig a deep enough hole, put in some compost, then water in the hole, put the plant in the hole and gently scatter soil around the roots, press down firmly, top up with soil and water again. Water each day until the plants are established.

Weeds

Now that our plants are growing and our sowings are coming through, we must do regular weeding so that unwelcome plants do not become established. In autumn, we cleared the ground of difficult weeds by digging them out. These weeds might be dock (the leaves of which, rubbed on the spot, take the bite out of a nettle sting), couch grass, dandelion, dog's mercury (also known as ground elder), buttercup and bindweed. You must be meticulous in getting all bindweed and couch grass roots out. Even a little piece will grow if left in the ground. Assuming they are now cleared, the weeding we must do during the growing season is to stop the new germinating seeds in their tracks. To do this you use a hoe which slices the weed stems. The handle of a hoe is too long for children to use easily. Either cut them down or weed by hand. Weeding of this kind has to be done regularly so that the weeds never really get established. Five minutes spent at the beginning of any gardening day is time well spent and it never then becomes a burden.

A Reflection on Weeds

There is, perhaps a sort of sacredness about weeds. Perhaps, if we could penetrate Nature's secrets, we should find that what we call weeds are more essential to the well-being of the world than the most precious fruit or grain.

Nathaniel Hawthorne, 1863

But what *is* a weed? Some children might say 'grass', but a grass lawn is not usually thought of as a mass of weeds. However, if there are daisies in amongst the grass they might be thought of as weeds. Yet if you grow a daisy in your garden, you wouldn't call it a weed but a plant, and you would take care of it. So weeds are really plants that, from our point of view, are in the wrong place.

Buttercup

Dock

Ground elder

From other points of view they are quite acceptable. For example, you might actually cultivate nettles on a spare bit of ground in order to provide the caterpillar of the Tortoiseshell butterfly with food. When we weed our garden, we destroy the plants we don't want because they compete with the plants we do want. The plants, generally acknowledged as weeds, certainly in a garden, are very successful as they are adapted to take over any vacant bit of ground for themselves and they can tolerate a wider range of circumstances than can more delicate plants. The children should learn to recognise at least the more common weeds likely to grow in their gardens.

Dandelions

A very common weed is the dandelion. But look at the beautiful seed-head it produces: a ball of little stars! You can now do the dandelion game. It would also be interesting for children to know where the name came from: 'Dents de Lion' (Lion's Teeth). Look at the ends of the petals of the flowers and you will see why.

Once the dandelions have seeded let the children hold a stalk and blow once, twice, three times and so on until all the seeds have blown away. Count how many blows it takes to send all the seeds on their way. The number of blows might even tell you the time of day.

The Dandelion clock is a funny kind of clock.
It doesn't say 'tick' and it doesn't say 'tock'.
It doesn't even chime, nor can it tell the time.
So it's up to you to find out!

B. Lockie

Weeds and Garden Plants that Feed Butterflies

There are five common and widespread butterflies. These are the Large and Small White, the Small Tortoiseshell, the Peacock and the Red Admiral. You may wonder why the Red Admiral is so called. Unfortunately, the story is not very exciting; the first entomologist to name the insect was apparently mis-heard when he exclaimed 'the Red Admirable'! But the wrong name stuck.

All the adults feed on the nectar of plants. Favoured plants include field scabious, Michaelmas daisy, purple loosestrife, nasturtium, wallflower, bramble, lavender, alyssum, honeysuckle, knapweed and buddleia. In autumn, Red Admirals gather in large numbers to feed on fallen and rotten fruit.

The caterpillars of the Large White are gregarious and can make an awful mess of your cabbages. Those of the Small are solitary and so do less damage. Both feed on the cabbage family, nasturtiums, and wallflowers.

The caterpillars of Small Tortoiseshell, Peacock and Red Admiral feed on stinging nettles. They are gregarious and sometimes eat all the leaves of the nettle plant leaving only bare stems.

Compost, Liquid Feeds and Manures

Making Compost

Any garden and household has a lot of organic waste and it would be criminal to throw it away. We can do much better than that. We can convert it into a rich compost which will feed plants and hold moisture. We do this by putting it in a composting box where the process of breakdown can take place. When the amount of waste in the box is right, and especially if you include some grass cuttings from the lawn, the compost-to-be will get so hot that you can hardly put your hand in it. It is this heat that kills weed seeds so that they are not brought back into the garden. Most people call this a 'compost heap' but it is more fun and descriptive to call it a 'garden cooker'.

In order to convert the waste we make a wooden box in a shady corner of the garden. The strong wooden box needs to be quite big. If too small, it won't heat up and, if too large, you will never be able to fill it up in reasonable time and, again, it will not get hot. A reasonable size would be a square metre and 1m high (3 x 3 x 3').

Compost heap or cooker

The box has no bottom so that earthworms can get in later and further break down the compost; this also allows the box to drain. One side should have moveable slats to allow easy access in order to turn the compost over and allow air in to help the process. Almost anything organic can go into the cooker: all the trimmings and peelings from the vegetables and fruit we eat, coffee grounds, tea bags (opened up), crushed egg-shells, lawn clippings, even the fluff and hairs from the vacuum cleaner, all the cleanings from the garden including most weeds. It is probably best not to include weeds that are seeding just in case your cooker does not get hot enough to kill them; and you should not include the roots of such pernicious weeds as couch grass, dock, dandelion, dog's mercury, buttercup and bindweed (convolvulus). If you have access to lots and lots of fallen leaves, you might consider making a separate composter for leaf mould. If you only have smaller quantities, include them in your compost heap.

If you don't have enough material for your cooker, you can ask other gardeners if they have waste they do not want. You can get the children to bring the refuse from their households to add to your cooker. You should not include left over cooked food and fat as this may attract rats. Nor should you include potato peelings, as these may carry one or more of the many potato diseases, particularly scab.

You must look after the cooker of course, because it is a living thing. If it gets too dry in summer, wet it with the watering can. In fact, if you use dilute liquid feed (see below) it will help the breakdown process. If it gets too soggy, mix in some dry material or shredded brown paper. It is best to have a roof on the cooker so that the wetness is under your control. In winter, it can be kept warm with old blankets. It is important to turn the compost once every month to let air into the system and also so that the outer part is moved to the centre. The bacteria that break down vegetable matter need air to work well. The final result will be sweet-smelling. However, if breakdown proceeds without air, then the result can be wet and smelly.

If you do all these things, you will get a wonderful reward next spring. All your weeds and throw-away materials will have turned into a beautifully rich compost that plants love. Then you can spread your home-made compost around the growing plants in your garden. They will be grateful and will reward you with splendid vegetables and flowers. Happy cooking!

Liquid Feeds

You can also make your own liquid feed for growing plants. Fill a bucket one third full with sheep droppings, nettle leaves, comfrey leaves or sea-weed, cover with water and leave for a week to ferment. The resulting liquid, although smelly, is an excellent liquid feed. It will stop being smelly once it is used on the plant. But you must dilute it before use, say a cupful to a gallon of water. Pour it around the plant. Liquid feeds are absorbed by the roots of plants over several days. If a dilute feed is sprayed on the leaves, it will be absorbed by the leaves within hours. However, it must be very dilute, say half or even less than that given to the roots.

Manures

Manures are usually animal-based and as they often come from stable or cowshed they are mixed with straw. It is best to let manure rot down before spreading it on the ground; but if you cannot do this spread it on the ground anyway and earthworms will draw it into the soil over the winter.

Poultry manure is very strong and needs to be mixed with vegetable matter and allowed to rot for some months. If you use it fresh it may scorch the plants it comes in contact with. If you have any choice, horse manure is the best.

Animals: Friends or Foes?

How might we put ideas about animal friends and animal foes across to small children? They still, thankfully, love the world around them and all that is in it and so you must try to get yourself on to that level. Even when considering pests therefore, you should approach them with reverence and understanding; there may be other ways of dealing with them than by killing them. After all, pests, like weeds, are something in the wrong place at the wrong time. They are not something to be stamped on and destroyed but rather admired, like all of nature.

The rest of this section describes some pests and some animal friends in a way that you might put to a small child, the aim being to give a balanced picture of the creatures that share the garden with us.

On a rainy day we can learn more about the animals that share the garden with us. They are all God's creatures and we must be kind to them. Of course, there are animals that like to nibble at what you have taken such care to grow: your flowers and vegetables. But, how can we be kind to them?

Let us look at **caterpillars** first. See how many there are on the cabbages. They can crawl from one cabbage to another too easily. What can we do? Yes, we can plant them farther apart. Always remember to plant your cabbages far apart; one huge step apart will do, even when they are small. In the meantime, we visit our garden every day to take the caterpillars away. You might make a nice game of it and see who can gather most. You can bring them to a nice big field where they can have many adventures and meet new friends.

Where do these caterpillars come from? They come from the Cabbage White Butterfly which lays its eggs on the cabbage family of plants (cabbage, broccoli, brussel sprouts). When the eggs hatch they grow into caterpillars which have enormous appetite for cabbages. This is one butterfly that is not welcome in the vegetable garden. You can keep the butterflies off by protecting the plants with a fine net. Hold the net tightly against the ground so that little birds don't get under and get tangled.

Then, there are the big, fat, slimy **slugs**. They are black and shiny and oh so sticky. What do they like to eat? They love to eat soft, juicy leaves and stems. And to help them do this, they have a long tongue like a rough file (much rougher than your pussy cat's tongue). So, in the night when no one is about to disturb them, they file away at the plants you most want to keep. Where do they like to live? For a start, they don't like the sun for it dries them out and they only feel comfy when they are damp. So, they look for the damp darkness underneath plants. If we make sure there is enough dry earth between what we grow, and even cover it with something that feels tickly to their foot such as pine needles and eggshells, or something that feels unpleasant to their skin, like coarse kitchen salt, they will go away. You can buy various copper bands and mats from garden centres that slugs do not like to cross to get at your tender plants. These kinds of animals don't have noses as we do but, even so, they can feel well or unwell and, if they feel uncomfortable somewhere, they just glide away. Some people put out the skin of orange or grapefruit between the plants that slugs like because, although they cannot smell, they don't like the feel of these fruits and stay away. Or you can make shelters that are cosy and damp for slugs and attract them there. Then you can gather them up and take them somewhere else far away from your garden. Such cosy places are upside down flower pots or a stone with a hollow underneath. Hedgehogs love to eat slugs. They do their good work while you are asleep. Ducks and frogs also eat them.

Controlling Slugs

Slugs are such destructive pests in some gardens that a whole section of The Organic Gardening Catalogue (see References) is devoted to them. Many of these methods kill the slugs although no bodies may be found except with sunken jars (see below). You may not wish to be involved in killing. Certainly, the philosophy of this book is to love all of nature. If this is how you feel, then go for the methods mentioned above, which simply (hopefully!) deter them.

We can use a natural enemy. This is called biological control and it can be very effective. 'Nemaslug' is the trade name for a preparation of very small worms (nematode worms) which enter the slug and introduce a bacterium which kills the slug. The preparation is mixed with water and sprayed on the ground from a watering can. It is harmless to all but slugs and lasts for six weeks.

Two kinds of pellets are available which are harmless to people, pets and wildlife. The first is called 'Advanced slug-killer rainproof pellets' and the other is 'Slug Stoppa' granules.

You can also attract slugs to jam jars sunk to their rims in the soil and filled with beer or milk. The dead bodies can be recycled by feeding them to robins and other birds on the bird table.

The Earthworm

Worms are great workers. They help us to dig the earth and, in doing so, they turn earth into a fine soil that plants can thrive on. Take a good look at him because like everything else he is really very beautiful. A worm is a bit like a small snake although he cannot bite. Just look at all these rings and on each is a line of tiny bristles that help the worm to move along. On a quiet night on the lawn you can actually hear these bristles rasping against the soil as the big earthworms pull leaves into their burrows. And sometimes there is a pink ring around his middle. This is his wedding ring. He only wears it when he is about to get married. It is amazing how birds eat worms and worms eat earth and earth grows vegetables and we enjoy eating our vegetables, don't we? Or would you rather eat some earth for dinner tonight?

In your compost heap there will be other kinds of worms (called Brandling worms). If your Daddy or your brother like fishing this is where they will go to collect worms and they will put them into a little tin box which they carry with them when they go fishing. And there you have it again: the fish eats the worm and the boy eats the fish: that is how it is.

Earthworms burrow about in the soil thus aerating and draining it; in that they could be bracketed, philosophically, with the moles. But unlike the moles they eat earth... and most of the bulk is passed out, being deposited as worm casts... Each acre of cultivated land has about 50,000 earthworms. Each worm deposits about seven ounces of dung per year so that the total weight of worm casts will be 10 tons per annum.

Edward Hyams, in Soil and Civilisation, *after Charles Darwin*

Beetles

Some of these are useful in the garden. They think that they are the best tidiers in the world for they keep feasting on dead things that have dropped on to the earth such as dead flowers, leaves or rotten fruit and, as there are always lots of these things lying about, it keeps them very busy. Ladybirds are helpful beetles as they eat aphids which suck the juice out of plants and so make them die.

Ladybird

There are also beetles which eat things they should not in the garden. One of these is the Click Beetle which usually lives in grassy fields where its caterpillar, called the wireworm, eats the roots of grasses. But sometimes it finds its way into your garden where it makes holes in potatoes. Potatoes are a nice change from boring old grass! There are also tiny slugs that love to feed on potatoes when they are lying in the potato bed. They make tiny tunnels, rather like those of wireworms, and they creep inside and start eating. Sometimes they leave nothing but the skin. There is not much you can do about wireworms and these slugs except to take your potatoes out of harm's way as soon as you can.

Birds

In spring, do you watch the birds? They all have different colours and shapes and sizes of nest and there are also differently coloured eggs. How clever they are at weaving nests out of grass, heather, rushes, feathers, moss and sometimes even mud.

Thrush

When the young are in the nest you can see the parents flying backwards and forwards with their beaks full of wriggly things and, if you listen carefully, you can hear the babies calling for food as soon as they hear their parents arriving. And, if you are still watching, you may see the parent birds fly out with the dirty nappies. Birds feed their young not only on earthworms, caterpillars and beetles but also on the small white or green bugs that you sometimes see on flowers: greenfly, whitefly and blackfly. There is a particular bird that loves blackfly and it is good to have him around. He is called the Bullfinch. I don't know why he has that name for he is not the least bit like a bull, but he is very beautiful with lots of pale red on his front and a black head. The Robin Redbreast is just like his name. The Robin is not at all shy. While you are working in the garden, he often comes down and sits quite near and as soon as his wee brown eyes spot a worm or an insect, hop, he is down beside you and it is gone. He often rewards you with his beautiful song. It is very cheerful to have him for company.

Robin

The Yellowhammer's Nest

A little boy was out for a walk in the country with his father. The father, who had been a bird-watcher in his youth, found a yellowhammer's nest. Now, yellowhammer's eggs have different markings from those of most other birds' eggs; they have squiggles and lines and dots rather than blotches and smears. The father showed the boy the nest in the hedge. The boy looked and shouted 'Dad, Dad, it's the Hindustani bird. What do the squiggles and lines mean? The father said he had no idea. The boy thought for a moment and said, 'I know. They say, please leave my eggs to grow into more Hindustani birds. Can we come again to see them?' 'Of course', said the father.

Next weekend they came back. The eggs were gone but, in their place, were four pink babies covered in sparse down. They had big heads and their eyes were closed. But when the boy gently tapped the edge of the nest, all four threw themselves up and opened their mouths wide thinking it was the parents and hoping to be the first to get food.

A week later the boy and his father were back. The baby birds had grown some feathers and their wing feathers were bursting out of sheaths. Their eyes were now open and they eyed the boy and his father with suspicion. In another seven days the babies had become fully feathered young birds and they filled the nest to overflowing. In fact, the nest had had to stretch to hold the growing family.

On the next visit the nest was empty. The young yellowhammers had flown. The boy was sad and glad at the same time.

It is interesting to think of the tiny happenings that lead to big consequences. The sight of the eggs of the 'Hindustani' bird triggered in the boy a passion for nature that led to a career as an ecologist.

Summer

The Summer Harvest

Summer is the time for soft fruits and flowers as well as vegetables such as broad beans, runner beans, garden peas, Swiss chard, spinach, herbs and summer turnips. How can we use this harvest and how can we save it for later when we have too much now?

Soft Fruits

Soft fruit of Summer includes raspberries, red, black and white currants, strawberries, gooseberries and blueberries. All can, of course, be eaten with cream or ice cream straight from the bush. In good years, however, you may not be able to eat all that is picked. The surplus can be made into jams and jellies which can also form the basis of cake fillings and tarts.

Jam and Jelly Making

This needs containers with tight-fitting tops. These jars with their tops have to be sterilised in boiling water and the hot liquid poured in and sealed while still hot. More than this, jam and jelly need a lot of sugar because sugar inhibits the growth of bacteria and moulds. Jams that contain less than the recommended amount of sugar will not keep for more than a few months. There is a lot of heat involved in the later stages of jam making and it is best to keep children well away. However, they can help with preparation and stirring in the early stages. Then, sit them at the kitchen table with paper and crayons to draw something of harvesting and storing and jam-making. They can also make labels with the name of contents, date and the child's name. These bottles can be used as a Christmas present for someone they love.

In making jam, select ripe but not over-ripe fruit; prepare the fruit by washing, if necessary, and by removing stems and bits and pieces. Note the amount of water needed for the fruit you are using according to the table below. Put the fruit and water in a large pan and bring to simmering; continue until the fruit is tender. Add the sugar, stirring until completely dissolved. Then, increase the heat and boil rapidly until the jam sets. You test this by pouring a little on to a saucer; allow to cool and if ready the jam will congeal and form a skin. Continue boiling rapidly until this point is reached. If you have added too much water, you will have to boil it off and too much boiling reduces the freshness of the resulting jam. When ready allow the jam to cool a little then pour it into warm sterilised jars set on a wet cloth and seal immediately.

Proportions of water and sugar to each pound of fruit.

Fruit	Water	Sugar
Blackberry and Apple	none	1 lb (0.45 kg)
Blackcurrant	$1/2$ pint (0.285 litres)	1 lb
Gooseberry	$1/4$ pint (0.143 litres)	1 lb
Rhubarb	none	1 lb
Strawberry	none	1 lb
Raspberry	none	1 lb
Damson	none	1 lb

Unboiled Raspberry Jam

Prepare and weigh the raspberries. Place in a pan and crush with a fork or potato masher. Bring to the point of boiling, add the sugar and stir until dissolved. Bring back to the point of boiling. Remove from the heat and pour into sterilised, warm jars. Seal immediately. Unboiled jam preserves the taste of the fruit better than boiled jam; it also preserves vitamins, especially vitamin C, which boiling destroys. However, unboiled jam may not last as long as boiled, although the sugar content in both acts as a preservative.

The setting of jam is due in part to a substance called pectin. This, together with the correct amount of sugar and some acidity, plays a role in the setting. Slightly unripe fruit has most pectin, and this diminishes as the fruit ripens. Over-ripe fruit has low levels of pectin and so will not easily set unless you use commercial pectin (see below).

Fruits naturally rich in pectin include: tart apples, blackberries, crab apples, cranberries, red and black currants, gooseberries, lemons, loganberries and plums (except Italian plums). Fruits low in pectin include: raspberries, apricots, blueberries, cherries, figs, peaches, pears, pineapple, rhubarb, strawberries, greengages and Italian plums.

The fruits with little pectin can be mixed with those which contain a lot, e.g. apple and pear. Or to keep the fruit pure you can add a commercial pectin which includes acidity (available from supermarkets, health food shops and chemists).

Mistakes to avoid in making jam

1. Avoid over-ripe fruit.
2. Avoid boiling the jam before the sugar has dissolved; this will make the sugar crystallize.

3. After the sugar is dissolved, boil rapidly.
4. Let the jam cool slightly before putting in jars; this will prevent the fruit from rising to the surface, especially with strawberries.
5. Don't put hot jam into cold jars.
6. Be sure to label the jars.

Flowers

Flowers can be dried and used for making greetings cards (see p.20). They can also be used to decorate salads and other dishes; indeed, some can be eaten as part of a salad, e.g. nasturtium, borage and calendula.

The flowers of the elder bush occur all over the countryside and in gardens and make a lovely syrup with a delicate taste. The syrup needs to be diluted with water or even better with fizzy water. The taste is not lessened but the fizz gives a little boost to the drink.

Elder Flower Syrup

Cut the bunches of white flowers when they are freshly opened and the petals are not falling freely. Collect them preferably on a sunny day. Put all the bunches into a bucket or similar and cover with cold water. Leave to steep for 24 hours and strain the mixture. Boil the clear liquid; add 1lb of sugar to every pint of the liquid (450g to 425ml), stirring until completely dissolved. Add a little lemon juice or citric acid crystals. Bring back to boiling briefly then pour into warm sterilised bottles or jars.

Rose hips too are ripening towards the end of Summer. They make a lovely syrup rich in vitamin C.

Rose Hip Syrup

Proceed as for jam and boil until the hips are a mush, then strain. Bring the liquid to boiling and add sugar as for elder flower syrup (1lb sugar [0.45kg] to 1 pint liquid [0.570 litres]) and stir until completely dissolved. Bring back to the boil briefly, then pour into sterilised and warm containers.

Deep freezing is another way to preserve soft fruits. However, not all fruits freeze well. Those that do are: raspberry, gooseberry, and black, red and white currants, and blueberries. These fruits retain much of their plumpness and taste after defrosting. Strawberries can be frozen but tend to collapse into a mush when defrosted. However, if you don't need them to look fresh and rounded, then freezing is quite satisfactory. Put the fruit in sealed containers or plastic bags to stop the fruit from losing moisture.

Vegetables

Lettuce, Swiss chard, spinach and summer turnip cannot be stored well and have to be eaten fresh. Therefore to avoid a glut that you cannot cope with, you need to make small sowings successively. Then you will extend the season and will have enough but not too much at any one time.

Broad beans, runner beans and garden peas can also be sown successively but this is not so important as these vegetables will freeze satisfactorily. Some of the crop can also be dried and saved for planting next year.

The Medicinal Properties of Plants

Plants have been used for thousands of years to cure and ease ailments. It is interesting to ask yourself how the usefulness of a plant might originally have been discovered. Was it trial and error? If so, an awful lot of people must have been ill at one time or another because many plants are poisonous. Did someone just happen to chew the bark of willow only to find that it eased his pain? Willow bark contains the active ingredient of aspirin.

Herbal Remedies

These flourished in the 17th and 18th centuries and form the basis of modern homeopathy, to which more and more people are turning as an adjunct to conventional medicine. There are now even books on veterinary herbal medicines, that is, herbal remedies for our pets.

Here are some commonly used plants that you can pick and use yourself. You should consult your doctor before you begin any herbal remedy and keep your doctor informed of the herbal remedies you are taking.

Dock or Docken (One old-fashioned name from Somerset, England is actually 'Doctors' Medicine'): takes the pain out of a nettle sting; rub the leaf on the sting.

Sage: used as a tea against sore throat and as a compress on a bruise to reduce pain.

Lemon Balm (Mellissa): as an infusion or tea, it is good for sore tummies.

Chamomile: soothing as a tea for sore tummies, especially cramp, and also as a compress held against the ear lobe, for ear ache.

St. John's Wort (Hypericum): as an infusion or tea against depression, especially in winter.

Thyme: as an infusion or tea against coughs.

Peppermint: as an infusion against coughs and colds and to settle spasm in an acid tummy.

Lime Blossom: as an infusion against fever.

Fennel Seed and **Aniseed**: as an infusion or tea against wind.

For all these remedies, if you are making an infusion or tea, take a small amount of fresh or dried leaves, pour boiling water over them in a cup and leave standing for three minutes before drinking. Blossom should preferably be picked in sunshine then dried and kept in air-tight containers in the dark.

The Song of the Self Heal Fairy

When little Elves have cut themselves,
And Mouse has hurt her tail,
Or Froggie's arm has come to harm,
This herb will never fail.
The Fairy's skill can cure each ill,
And soothe the sorest pain.
She'll bathe and bind and soon they'll find,
That they are well again.

Cicely Mary Barker

For a compress or poultice take a small quantity of flowers or leaves and wet them with a little boiling water. Place it between muslin and cover, if necessary, with a thicker material. Apply to the affected part.

Here are uses for some other herbs:

Lavender can be made into lavender bags and put into a linen cupboard to keep the air fresh. First make some muslin bags with a woollen tie threaded through the open end. Then, pick lavender flowers, preferably on a sunny day. Dry them on a sheet of paper in a warm room or very low oven. When dry, pack into muslin bags and tie tightly.

Mint leaves can be dried and hung in the kitchen to keep flies away.

Herbs and the Smelling Game
This is a fun game. Once the children have become familiar with herbs
and their healing powers, you can let them sniff the herbs and later
either blind-fold or simply with eyes shut, present some herbs for
smelling. Some, such as mint, lemon balm and chives are easy to guess.
Then try more difficult herbs such as thyme. Then go on to still more
difficult ones like lovage, sage and parsley.

Companion Plants

Some plants grow better in the presence of others; some plants keep
pests away from others. We call these plants 'companion plants'. There
are too many examples of companion plants to do justice to the subject
but here are some examples (see also Bob Flowerdew and Jacqui Hurst
in the References).

Wild garlic keeps aphids off roses and fruit trees.
Chives work against black spot on roses and scab on apples.
French marigold (Tagetes) works against the potato eel worm.
Tomatoes and **carrots** seem to grow better together.

We might try to put the idea of companion plants over to the small
child, remembering that for him to grasp the concept it must be
presented in language and images that connect with his experience.

Now, here is something that the plants want to tell us. They are just like us in
that they like to be with their friends. You know how you feel more
comfortable with some people rather than with others. Well, some plants grow
best when they are close to their friends. For instance, strawberries like to be
beside lettuce and radish but not beside beans and cabbages, when they just
won't grow so well. There are also special flowers which are like nurses
because they look after other plants. Marigolds protect potatoes by stopping
tiny animals from eating them.

    People who lived long ago were closer to nature than we are today and
knew more of her secrets. But we can learn. If you were to visit an old-
fashioned garden you might see rows of these flowers in use; and by the front
door, rowan trees to welcome the fairies.

Rowans around the door

Propagation: More than Two for the Price of One

Earlier we spoke of tubers, bulbs and corms as ways by which plants can make more of themselves (see p.21) These are clones of the original plant. There are still more ways by which this can be done: by cuttings, layering, division and off-sets from bulbs. This is a fascinating aspect of gardening which gives you as many new plants as you want. All this can be done by children and it seems quite miraculous that a bare stick stuck in the ground can produce a new plant. You have to be patient because it may take some time, from a few months to two years.

Because it takes longer than germinating a seed, how do you put this over to small children so that you hold their attention? One way is to hark back to what they have already experienced in this way.

Do you remember going out in spring and finding pussy willow and catkins of hazel, alder and birch? Do you remember you brought them inside and put them in water in a vase; and you decorated them with daffodils? They looked beautiful and they lasted quite a long time. The daffodils were the first to fade and be put on the 'garden cooker'; and later, when the catkins faded, you were going to do the same with them. But did you look at them before you threw them out? What did you see? Yes, some of the twigs had grown roots out into the water in the vase. They were real roots although easily broken because they had not grown in the earth where they should have been. Here we have a chance to build a small shelter for a sensitive plant, or a hedge to protect your garden from winds. Just dig a hole, gently place the stem with roots on the hole and fill up with soil. Water your new plant even if it doesn't look much now. It will grow strong roots and above ground it will turn into a plant just like its mother. You may have to give your new plant a crutch at first so that it does not fall over in the wind. You do not always have to grow the roots in a jar; push the stem into the ground, keep it moist, and it will grow roots. In this way you can make a hedge for free! It is called, in grown-up language, 'Propagation'.

Cuttings

These can consist of a length of stem with or without leaves, a section of root, a single leaf or a bud. How you deal with the cutting varies a little from plant to plant but there are rules that apply to all. For a cutting to produce roots it must have light (but not direct sunlight), warmth, moisture and air. The medium you put the cutting into is a mixture of compost, sharp sand and perlite. The perlite got from garden centres is inert but holds moisture. The mix is free-draining yet it holds moisture and lets air in. Alternatively you may push hardwood cuttings directly into the soil.

Willows are typical hardwood cuttings taken in autumn and early winter. Cut the stem into 20cm (8") sections. At the top end cut the stem horizontally and at the other end cut the stem diagonally. If you are planting a lot this makes sure which end is which. Then scrape a little bit of bark off the sharp end to make a wound; this helps rooting. This cutting now gets pushed into the ground, watered and then you wait. In spring it will begin to shoot and may make as much as a half metre in the first year. You may prefer to push the cuttings into a pot with the compost mixture and care for them until they form roots when they can be planted out. To make a small sheltering hedge, you simply push the cuttings in 10cm (4″) apart in a double line. Trim, if necessary, in late summer. Fast growing willows to use are the osier and the violet willow which has beautiful chestnut-coloured stems in winter (see Edgar Watts in References). You can make a living domed willow house using long stems which curve over and are tied together.

Willow fence

Willow gazebo – winter

Willow gazebo – summer

You may also take semi-mature cuttings from shrubs in mid-summer. These are best taken by pulling them off the stem leaving a 'heel' of bark. With pyracantha and ceanothus it is essential to have this heel or no roots will grow. In summer you can propagate herbaceous plants by using shoot tips or a single bud with a leaf attached. All should be grown in the compost mixture and it is absolutely vital to keep them moist.

Layering
This takes advantage of the fact that the branches of many plants when touching the ground send out roots and produce a new plant. Forsythia, weeping willow, clematis, bramble (blackberry), rhododendron and many others will root in this way. Brambles root in a few months but others take two years so you may have to be patient.

Layering

The method is to bring the branch down to the ground and, where it touches, scratch a small wound in the stem. Then dig a hole, put this part of the stem in and fill up with soil. Peg the branch down or put a flat stone on top. When it has rooted, cut it free from the parent plant but leave it in the ground until autumn before transplanting.

Bulbs

If left untended in the ground, bulbs eventually produce a great mass of little bulbs (offsets) and because they are crowded they don't grow so well. It is good, therefore, to split up these bulbs every few years and plant them elsewhere.

Herbaceous Plants

These, similarly, grow into a dense mass of roots and may come to dominate the part of the garden that they are in. You can divide the clump into four or more parts by wrenching it asunder using two garden forks back to back. Or you can simply cut them using a sharp spade. Each part with its roots can be planted elsewhere.

Separating herbaceous plants

Angels and fairies

In our modern world, angels and fairies are often regarded as childish fictions. But for small children angels are a reality. Even those who have never been told about angels immediately open to their 'being'. Of course, if you don't have a sense of such things yourself, there is no point in talking to children about them. But it does give children a very safe and protected feeling to talk about angels almost daily. If you can relate to such ideas you can tell children about their own guardian angel who cares for and guides each person. You cannot see angels but you can sense them.

You can tell them about the different angels who have different tasks, for instance those who specially look after plants, others who look after animals and those who perhaps guide people across the road at a dangerous crossing (but this doesn't replace taking due care of course!). You can incorporate poems about angels in the kindergarten routine, for example perhaps saying this well-known verse when the dolls are put to sleep.

Mathew, Mark, Luke and John,
Bless the bed that I lie on,
Four corners to my bed,
Four Angels there are spread,
One at my head and one at my feet
And two to guard me as I sleep.
God within and God without,
And Jesus Christ all round about.
If any danger come to me,
Sweet Jesus Christ deliver me.
Before I lay me down to sleep
I give my soul to Christ to keep.
And, if I die before I wake,
I pray that Christ my soul will take.
Amen.

Anon

It is a good idea to have a picture of an angel in the kindergarten or perhaps a book with pictures of different angels – for instance, of 'Tobias and the Angel' and also the many Annunciation paintings by artists of the Renaissance.

Fairies are perhaps a more approachable subject than angels. All children and grownups know about fairies. The well-known 'Fairies of the Flowers' books by Cicely Mary Barker are widely available. Be sure you get the genuine article; there are some poor imitations. Each painting of fairies is accompanied by a poem.

As I have said, angels and fairies are a reality for small children. If possible we should encourage this, for dismissing otherworldly realities can inflict hurt on a small child, who has a more 'universal' awareness than the often more materialistic adult. Here is a poem in which childish wonder and imagination is contrasted with matter-of-factness and even cynicism.

One day when we went walking,
I found a Dragon's tooth,
A dreadful Dragon's tooth.
'A Locust thorn', said Ruth.

One day when we went walking,
I found a Brownie's shoe
A Brownie's Button shoe.
'A dry pea pod', said Sue.

One day when we went walking,
I found a Mermaid's fan,
A merry Mermaid's fan.
'A scallop shell', said Dan.

One day when we went walking,
I found a Fairy's dress,
A Fairy's flannel dress,
'A mullein leaf', said Bess.

Next time that I go walking,
Unless I meet an Elf,
A funny, friendly Elf,
I'm going by myself!

Valine Hobbs

Are Fairies True?

Young children rarely ask at the end of a fairy story, 'Is it really true?'. But, if they did, the answer must be, 'Yes, of course it is true'. You can say this because, whatever you yourself may believe, this answer is required by the consciousness of the small child. And also because fairy-tales do indeed contain truths about human life embodied in wonderful imagery and metaphor. The small child is at one with the world of magic and nature, and this includes fairies, gnomes and angels. As the child moves into further phases of development, fairies make way for other images. However, the fact that these have lived with them during the appropriate stage of their development means that that stage has been fully realised and satisfied; and they are ready to move on in an emotionally healthy way. There is no question of disillusionment. So, to say to a small child that fairies are true is not lying to them; they are true at that stage of the child's development. In your stories, therefore, if you enter fully and imaginatively into the fairy realm, you will at the same time enter the stage of consciousness of the children in your care.

Midsummer

Just as midwinter is exciting with early dark and candles, so is midsummer an exciting time with so much light. Here it is not dark until ten or eleven o'clock and farther north, hardly at all.

This is a time when it is easy to 'fly away' and it is difficult to concentrate and be inward. If grown-ups experience this, how much more do small children? All the more reason to keep the structure and rhythm of the day and of the week going strongly. If possible, arrange a rest hour. It gives the children a little time away from the exhausting light. If they can fall asleep, fine, but if not at least they should have a quiet hour sitting on their bed with a book. This also gives the mother or carer a chance to rest or, if inclined, a chance to get on with chores. After this siesta, have something to eat and drink and then all can get through the rest of the day with renewed energy.

Midsummer's day, 21st June, is a special day for the fairies, a day when human beings should be more aware of them than at any other time. We can make a 'fairy plate' to celebrate this. Fill a small, colourful plate with tiny goodies: chopped nuts, raisins, crumbs and little pieces of fruit. When all is prepared we walk to the 'fairy house' which is in the tangled roots of a fallen tree or an old gnarled tree with twisted roots which time has covered with mosses and ferns – the more mysterious the better.

As we get near to the 'house' a deep hush falls over the children and, without thinking, we all go on tip-toe.

'Why can't we see the Fairies?'
'Ah, I bet they're watching us'.
'I saw a little glitter'.
'Where?'.
'It must be hiding'.

With great reverence the offering is placed on what we are sure is their dining room and, after deciding what all the other spaces are used for, we creep quietly away. On the way home, we may gather flowers to decorate our own houses.

Here is a song to sing on the way back from leaving the plate of food.

Fairies, fairies, here is a surprise.
We hope you will like it.
It's for you to share.
Fairies, fairies, find your surprise.

B. Lockie

Fair – ies, fair – ies, here is a sur – prise.

We hope you will like it. It's for you to share.

Fair – ies, fair – ies, fi – nd your sur – prise.

We wait until the next day when we return to see if the fairies have found our gift and eaten it. The tension can be quite high. Yes, the plate is empty and beautifully cleaned. But, what is this? A little parcel wrapped up in leaves. It is a beautiful crystal probably found by the gnomes and given to the fairies on this special occasion.

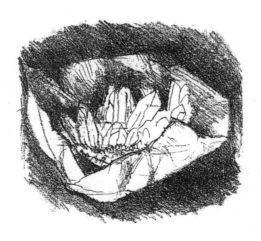

And another song, to the same music as above, after finding the crystal.

> Fairies, fairies, now it is our turn.
> Yes, we will like it.
> It's for us to share.
> Fairies, fairies, thank you for our surprise.
>
> *B. Lockie*

We thank the creatures of the wood. The children are deeply satisfied and walk home quite overcome. They show the crystal with great joy to everyone. As this happens only once each year, it is long looked forward to and long remembered.

Telling Animal Stories

When you talk about fairies and gnomes you bring the children into another realm, the realm of magic. The more stories of this sort that you tell children the more they are absorbed in a mood of awe and magic. In the same way, when we tell stories about animals we engender a feeling for animals, both those in the garden and also animals in general.

The Fables of Aesop are moral stories in which, more often than not, arrogance is humbled, as in 'The Grasshopper and the Ants', 'The Hare and the Tortoise' and 'The Stork and the Fox'. Or they may be about cleverness in animals; for example, 'How the Fox rid himself of Fleas'. The Aesop Fables are sometimes a little sparse in the telling and the moral is presented as though to an adult; but they provide a wonderful basis for the imaginative story-teller to expand in a way that suits small children. The 'Just So' stories of Rudyard Kipling are a delight too. Of course, these stories imbue animals with human attributes, thoughts and emotions. But if the aim is to get a message across and to entertain, then it is entirely justified and is in tune with the small child's view of the world.

Here is one such story:

The Lion and the Mouse
(An Aesop's fable retold by Beatrys Lockie)

King Lion was lying fast asleep. He had no enemies but Man, and his tummy was full. He was having a wonderful dream about chasing antelopes and the tip of his tail was twitching with excitement. Unknown to him a tiny mouse was watching this and, fascinated by the movement, sprang as if catching prey.

This woke the lion up and, in a moment he pounced and held the mouse in his mighty paw ready to crush him with his huge teeth. 'Oh please King Lion, dear King Lion, spare me. I meant you no harm. I was just playing. Besides, I am so small that you would hardly taste me. 'Oh no,' said King Lion, 'He who annoys the King shall pay for it.' 'Please, please have mercy on me. Who knows, I may save your life one day'. At this the King laughed heartily saying 'I very much doubt that'. But he let the mouse go.

Now, it was some months later that the mouse got his chance. As I mentioned before, the lion's only enemy was Man and there were those who had hunted him many times and in many ways. As this lion lived in a forest, the hunters decided to make a trap for him. They dug a deep pit and covered it with a net and then branches and leaves so that no one but the hunters could see that there was danger. And this is exactly what happened. The King of the Beasts stepped on the trap and it collapsed. The lion fell in with a great roar. He became entangled in the net and could not get out.

And who heard the roar? The mouse, of course. He thought 'My friend the lion is in danger. I must go to his aid'. And so, as fast as his little legs would carry him, he ran and ran until he found the source of the noise. 'Oh King, I have come to help you. You saved my life and now it is time for me to save yours.' If the circumstances had not been so serious the lion would have laughed. 'How on earth?' was all he could say. But the mouse answered 'I have very sharp teeth. Now, don't talk to me. I have work to do'.

Carefully the mouse stepped on to the net and began to chew. Quite soon there was quite a big hole in the net but not big enough to let the lion out. It was getting dark and the mouse knew that the hunters would soon be back to see what was in their trap. He redoubled his efforts and chewed and chewed until before long the hole was big enough to let the lion squeeze out. Just then they heard the hunters coming nearer. 'Quick, on my back', said the lion. And so the two escaped and stayed friends for the rest of their lives. And, to this day, a lion will never harm a mouse.

'And the Lion and the Mouse stayed friends for the rest of their lives.'

CHAPTER 5

The Town Child

Many town children have access to a garden. But by the term 'town child' I mean those children, perhaps in inner city areas, who are more or less surrounded by concrete, tarmac and stone and who have no easy access to a garden. Whatever facilities you may, or may not have, here is a lovely way to start the day.

Everyone has Weather! Starting the Day

Ask the children what kind of weather it is today. Once you have the correct answer, here is a song and some poems to suit. Of course, this applies to children anywhere not just those in city centres. But because town children are somewhat shielded from weather, it is a good thing to direct their attention to the weather environment in an enjoyable way.

Rainy Weather (song)

Pitter patter hear the rain,
Beating on the window pane.
Splashing, dashing, dripping down,
Wetting all the streets in town.
Boots are muddy and I get
Socks and shoes and feet all wet.
How it pelts and how it pours,
Hurry up and get indoors.

C. Kovacs

Pit – ter pat – ter hear the rain, Beat - ing on the win – dow pane.

Splash-ing, dash-ing, dripp – ing down, Wet – ting all the streets in town.

Boots are mud - dy and I get Socks and shoes and feet all wet.

How it pelts and how it pours, Hur - ry up and get in – doors.

Windy Weather (poem)

Have you seen the Wind?
Neither I nor you.
But, when the leaves are rustling,
The Wind is passing through.

Have you seen the Wind?
Neither you nor I.
But, when the trees are bowing down,
The Wind is passing by.

Christina Rossetti

Sunny Weather (poem)

Oh Sun we love you so,
Oh Sun we love you so.
You make us feel so good,
You make us grow,
And help to grow our food.
Oh Sun we love you so.

B. Lockie

Misty Weather (poem)

One misty, moisty morning
When cloudy was the weather,
There I met an old man
Clothed all in leather;

Clothed all in leather
With cap under his chin –
How do you do, and How do you do,
And How do you do again? (children shake hands)

Anon

The City Centre Garden

In the city centre is there a balcony or a yard? These obviously give
more floor space for pots and other containers. You may have only a
window-sill but you can still do a lot of gardening; and you can add
more space as you progress by erecting shelves inside and out and by
brackets from which to hang baskets and the bird bell (see p.38). One
just has to change one's approach a bit. Nearly all that has been
described already can be achieved in window boxes. There are, however,
some extra considerations because of the locality. Watering becomes
even more important because containers can dry out quite quickly. You
can slow up the loss of moisture by adding a little perlite to your
compost. Perlite is an inert substance which soaks up water and gives it
off slowly. It can be bought in garden centres. Your soil will come in a
bag in the form of compost from the garden centre. This means that
you will have no initial manuring although you will have to give a
liquid feed as the plants grow up. You will also have no initial weeding
to do, and compost from a bag is sterilised and therefore free of pests.

Containers

Containers you can use include the standard round clay or plastic pots in a great range of sizes and colours, and also rectangular window boxes.

But you can be imaginative and use more unusual containers, such as welly boots, old kettles and watering cans, and hollowed tree-stumps.

Some of these will need holes drilled in the bottom for drainage. Air bricks (bricks with holes in them) provide another possibility especially for house leeks and other sedums. Such bricks are even more attractive if they have been worn by the action of the sea or a river.

With an array of containers you can do almost all the sowing and planting described earlier and you can gauge how much you do to the space available and the time you have for tending. As already stated, watering will be an important activity and a valuable lesson for children to get it just right. It is important to remember that just because a window box is outside, it will not necessarily get enough moisture from rain. Walls often act as a shelter from rain and they retain heat so that the containers dry out more quickly. You will have to keep the compost damp, but never sodden. It is better to give a little often rather than a flood seldom. Later, as beans and potatoes grow up, they will need more food, which you can give as a liquid in their water about once a week. ('Tomorite' is commonly available in garden centres. It is an inorganic preparation for tomatoes but can also be used on plants in pots. It is well-balanced in terms of potash, nitrogen and phosphorus.) Many of the containers are best started indoors if you have a window ledge inside. If not, perhaps a shelf in front of the window or a tallish table.

Window boxes can be bought in many shapes, colours and sizes but they may be expensive. What about making them together? You don't need to be an expert joiner to nail straight pieces of wood together, and any activity like that inspires and enthuses a child. You can buy the wood but this too can be expensive. One of the advantages of living in town is that you have access to skips and they are often a great source of timber. You might even be lucky enough to find discarded window boxes. Best to ask permission from the owner of the skip first. The size of the box obviously depends on the size of the window-sill or shelf. If it is a long sill it might be best to make two or three boxes. Remember that when filled with damp compost they can be quite heavy. The deeper they can be the better. I suggest 22cm high (8½″). Drill holes in the bottom for drainage. If your sill slopes outwards you may need wedges to straighten the box so that it doesn't lean forward precariously. If your window sill is painted, put old saucers under the pots to stop the paint from peeling.

Plants for Containers

In planting up a window box, try to arrange for a succession of plants. You can do this by planting bulbs in two layers, hyacinths below and snowdrops above.

Cross section of window box

The snowdrops will flower first, and fade, and their place will be taken by the hyacinths. For flowers on top I suggest: lobelia which flowers from summer into autumn (there are several colours, blue, white and now reddish) or godetia (another long-flowering plant) and petunias and nasturtiums for hanging down. See the planting sketch overleaf.

Petunias will grow quite tall and sometimes need a support, so put them at the back. You could plant one or two small ivy plants in between; variegated ivy has beautiful leaves. In the pots on either side some herbs are lovely: chives, parsley, mint (there are many different kinds), lemon balm and thyme. You can make delicious tea with the three last.

Now for the inside window sill: radishes, cress, a small strawberry plant, a few carrots, a pea, a broad bean and two kinds of lettuce (Little Gem and the frilly Lollo Rosso perhaps). The inside containers will dry out more quickly than those outside and so need more careful watching and watering. The bean and pea will need some support.

Plan view of window box with plant contents

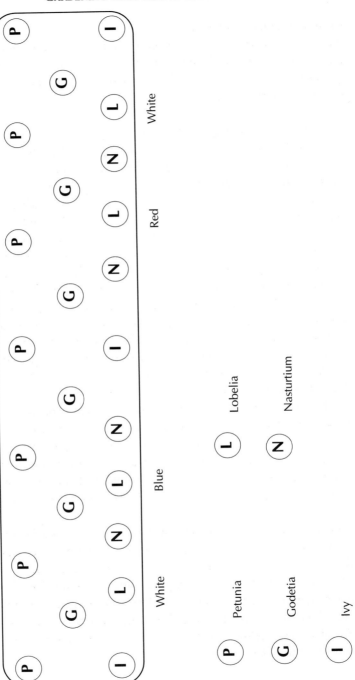

More Plants for Containers
Here are some additional things to grow in your containers. Some will need the warmth of indoors all the time because they come from warmer countries. Others will benefit initially but can be put outside later to make room for new plants.

Go to the greengrocer and get the following items: a carrot, a beetroot, a lemon, a pineapple, an avocado and a sweet potato. Take the carrot, beetroot and pineapple first. Cut the top off each, leaving about 2.5cm (1") of flesh. Plant the tops in dampened compost in a 12cm (4$^{1}/_{2}$") pot, so that the compost just comes up to the cut portion. Place indoors and keep damp. The cuttings will root and grow leafy tops; that of beetroot is crinkly, and red and green, while that of carrot is fine, feathery and pale green. Most people throw away the top of a pineapple. Don't. Treat it in the same way as the beetroot and carrot and it, too, will sprout. It will need more heat than the others though.

Now try the avocado. Find an egg-cup and fill it with water. Put the avocado, thick end downwards, into the egg-cup, but suspended just *above* the water. If the girth of the avocado doesn't allow it to sit neatly, try propping it up with tooth-picks. In warmth, the roots will soon sprout downwards to the water and a shoot will appear at the pointed end. When the roots are well-developed you can plant the avocado in damp compost, being very careful not to damage the delicate roots.

Next, lemon pips. Soak them for two days in water and then press them to a depth of 2.5cm (1") into damp compost. You won't get lemons but you will get a plant with glossy leaves. There is no need to sprout the sweet potato. Half bury it in damp compost and it will root and send shoots upwards which will need sticks or a net to climb on. Given good conditions, it will climb around your window and, in warmth, may even produce flowers.

You can also plant acorns and chestnuts and grow your own trees. Then find somewhere to plant the seedlings in the spring. You could become friends with a park keeper and he will show you the best place to put them. For sowing cress you can get delightful ceramic 'cress hedgehogs'. These have a section of spines omitted on top and in their place is a container. Fill the container and sow the cress. When it comes up, in a few days, and before you cut it for on a sandwich, the dense growth provides the missing spines.

A Garden on a Plate

This is what you will need:

- A large and deep soup plate or similar. It does not matter which colour or pattern as all will be covered.
- A moss of any kind. With moss you can create some ups and downs which makes the little garden more interesting. Take care not to pull the moss all from one place for that would leave an unsightly bare patch; just take a little here and there.
- Collect all sorts of things that your fancy dictates but they must be small and in proportion to the plate. I would choose a beautiful piece of bark, some small stones, a mirror, a little gnome; and for flowers, cut stems of yellow primroses 5cm (2″) high, forget-me-nots and a leafy plant like a decorative grass, a spray of ivy and some leaves of the dead nettle plant.

Moss garden

This is how you make the garden:

Cover the plate completely with moss and then, off centre, make a space and fit the mirror in to suggest a little pond. Now push the stems of the flowers into the moss carefully or they may break. It helps to use a match stick or tooth pick to make the holes. Arrange them in groups of uneven numbers (even numbers always look stiff and formal, odd numbers are more satisfying). Leafy plants can be shaped into a little grove. If you have a gnome, sit him beside the pond. The bark can be a little boat. Plants which are not yet flowering often have thick stems with buds e.g. aquilegia, the columbine. A small group will look like trees. Daisies look sweet against dark green moss. Once you get started you are spoilt for choice. Don't overdo it as the plate garden can soon look too full. Give the garden a little water to keep it fresh.

You have made a moss garden but you can make all sorts of themes on the plate. This is what you need to make a desert: sand, tiny stones, a sprouting pineapple top. a small cactus or a house leek, a make-believe snake, a bird's skull or other bits of skeleton, a bleached piece of wood and a small camel.

Desert garden

Or a seaside scene: sand, shells, a dried-up small fish, a small starfish and a small sea urchin, a bleached piece of wood and seaweed. A small mirror can suggest the sea edge and a little boat can be pulled up on the sand.

Seaside scene

These plates are lovely home-made presents for grannies and grandpas and other people you want to visit who might be in a nursing home or hospital.

City Expeditions

You may be able to make an expedition to a park or botanical garden. The park will have flowers and trees and shrubs. The kinds of trees all have different characteristics of shape, size, leaves, flowers and autumn colours. You can do a nice game and say 'Who does this tree remind you of? Is it like mummy or daddy, a fairy or a witch?' The oak is strong and firm and immovable. The larch is delicate, young and dancing. Trees also suggest moods. The yew looks sinister whereas the willows are joky fellows. There will be a succession of flowers in the park. First of all come snowdrops then the yellow celandine and willow catkins; then come daffodils – and then it is spring.

The botanical garden may have greenhouses that represent different climates. You can travel from tropical rainforest to desert and experience the different climates and the different kinds of plants associated with each. You cannot go very far with all this for a three to four-year-old, but the experience is well worthwhile. The desert climate is hot and very dry and many of the plants look a bit dried up; others, like cactus, are often quite fleshy, so much so that they are a source of water (or at least some moisture) for thirsty travellers. The rainforest is hot and humid. Everything drips with water and there is a strong smell of damp compost in the air. The plants often have enormous leaves that are used to thatch huts.

Often there are derelict sites in cities where you will find tough pioneering plants which can colonise bare inhospitable ground, and don't have to struggle with other plants for light. The pioneers include fireweed (willow herb), dandelion and thistle. The bomb-sites from the Second World War were quickly taken over by willow herb, whose seeds can travel for miles on the wind. Thistles and dandelions also have little parachutes on their seeds so that they too can float for miles.

There are also mammals, notably the fox, which find a safe haven in derelict sites in cities. They scavenge the refuse from houses and restaurants and seem to live quite successfully. You may get a glimpse of one even by day but mostly they are secretive and appear at night.

Allotments

At the beginning of the 1939-45 war I was moved to yet another school because we had to move house. I was not at all happy at the new school because the class was already a unit and I did not fit in. However, across the road from the school were allotments and it was part of the curriculum that each child of the class I was in was allowed to have a plot of land. We had a wonderful teacher, a Mr. Beech, who not only understood children of our age but also was a fount of knowledge; he was patient and knew just when to leave us free.

So, I cultivated my little plot whenever I was able and, as it was war-time, it was a bonus to be able to bring some food home. I could see my plot from the class-room window and when I felt unhappy, my eyes would wander over the road to my flowers and vegetables and that was my solace. I sat there and willed the vegetables to grow! I grew rhubarb, cress, radishes, several kinds of lettuce and later, broad beans and peas. At weekends the gates were open at 7am and I was there again with flask and sandwiches. Sometimes I took my mother and sister to see what I was growing on my land. I was so proud. My little allotment is one of my few good memories of those days.

There are allotments in nearly every town and these are used by people who may have no garden but who want to grow their own food and flowers. Visit their flower shows and harvest festivals and see what can be done in an allotment. Make friends with an allotment holder. All are keen gardeners and will probably enjoy the company, especially if you seem to be interested in what they are doing. You will learn a lot simply by watching and asking questions. As you learn more you can offer help. It would be a nice gesture then to take along a little jar of apple chutney that you may have made from the recipe given earlier. You will have made a real gardening friend.

Irene Remembers her Father's Allotment

When Irene was a little girl, she and her brother and sister were not allowed to go to the allotment with their father during the week because they had homework to do. But, come Saturday and Sunday, it was a feast to be invited, especially on warm, sunny days. Mother made a picnic. It was always grated cheese with chopped tomatoes. Even now, Irene associates the taste of cheese and chopped tomatoes with the feeling of pleasure at being in her father's allotment. And how much better everything tasted in the fresh air! There never seemed to be enough; they were always hungry.

There was a small, simple shed painted green and with windows to the south. Inside there were five folding chairs and a card table, a primus stove and the inevitable teapot, kettle and cups. (There must also have been the usual gardening tools but Irene doesn't remember them).

Except at meal-time there was no sitting around. What a lot they learned; composting, raking to a fine tilth, sowing carefully and covering over, watering, protecting against the wind and planting using a 'dibble' (a sharpened stick, often made from the handle and shaft of an old spade and used for planting potatoes, bulbs, and seedlings).

At the potato harvest, the father forked the potatoes out of the soil and the children scrabbled over the ground to pick them up. There was always a rush to get the most or the biggest. Irene is grateful for these wonderful working weekends and, now in her sixties, looks back to them with nostalgia. Her parents used to say how sorry they were for those poor children who had no interests and who hung about street corners looking forlorn.

Sunday mornings were for church but in the afternoon it was back to the allotment or collecting sheep droppings during a walk in the hills. The droppings were put in a bucket of water (rain water from a barrel) and mixed with a little soot and allowed to ferment. The diluted liquid was used to feed plants, especially leeks. As a child, Irene was always amazed and amused that leeks needed feeding just like herself.

My Garden

A garden is a lovesome thing, God wot!

Rose plot,

Fringed pool,

Fern'd grot.

The veriest school

Of peace; and yet the fool

Contends that God is not –

Not God! in gardens! when the eve is cool?

Nay, but I have a sign;

'Tis very sure that God walks in mine.

T.E. Brown, 1830-97

You may wish to acquire an allotment for yourself. They are usually owned and rented out – very cheaply – by the local council. Ask an allotment holder how to go about it. In any case, good luck and much happiness with your work, be it in town or country in window box or garden.

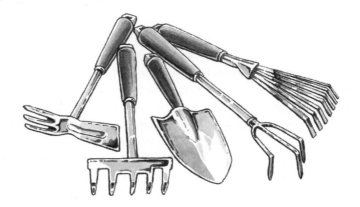

CHAPTER 6

The Gardener's Calendar

This book aims to help the adult guide young children through the gardening year. Of necessity I have concentrated on a limited number of easily grown plants and on the principle techniques of simple gardening. In this calendar of what to do and when, more plants and vegetables are introduced so that the adult can either choose alternatives or use a wider variety of plants. The timing of each activity has to be fairly general because of differing local climates. Some activities like hoeing, of course, transcend seasons and go on and on!

September

- Harvest, use and store vegetables and fruits. Make jams, jellies and chutneys.
- Collect, dry and store seeds for planting and to feed birds.
- Hoe weeds and continue at two-week intervals as weather permits.
- Plant crocuses and other bulbs inside in pots for winter flowering.
- Plant garlic, daffodils, crocuses, snowdrops, scylla and aconite outside for flowering in spring.
- Sow hardy annual flowering plants outside to overwinter.
- Turn the compost heap to let air in.
- Leave the tidying of herbaceous plants until early spring in order to give shelter and food to small birds and insects.
- Decrease water for all pot plants as the growth rate slows.
- Feed vigorous indoor pot plants eg. Christmas cactus and ficus (fig).
- Order seed catalogues, and catalogues for seed potatoes, and for herbaceous plants.

October

- Harvest and store root crops (carrots, potatoes, parsnips, turnips, garlic and onions).
- Spread mulches around established plants, trees and shrubs.
- Lime the future brassica beds (cabbage, broccoli, kale, brussel sprouts). Do not put manure on at the same time.

November-March

- Check stores and remove diseased items so that they do not infect others. Continue to inspect stores at monthly intervals through the winter.
- Collect up all prunings too woody for the compost heap and have a bonfire or shred for paths.
- Turn the compost heap to allow air in. Collect fallen leaves and garden waste and put in compost heap or gather around the base of trees and shrubs as a mulch. If you have lots of leaves you can make a separate heap for them.
- Order seeds, seed potatoes and herbaceous plants for the spring.
- Put out food and water for birds (bird bell, peanuts, fat balls and seeds in a suitable dispenser).
- Make traps for slugs and save plastic bottles to use as shelters (or cloches) for young plants in early spring. Save toilet roll centres for carrots against carrot fly.

Spring

- Check stores for diseased items.
- Put potatoes in a shallow box or egg box on a window-sill inside to sprout (called 'chitting').
- Continue to feed the birds, especially if spring is late.
- Keep hoeing as weather permits.
- Spread compost around growing plants.
- Sow inside any plants for later planting out, including brassicas, herbs and hardy and half-hardy annual flowering plants.
- As the soil warms up sow outside: peas, broad beans, onions, leeks, beetroot, kohlrabi, cabbage, cauliflower, broccoli, kale, lettuce, spinach, turnip, carrots, chards, parsnips, herbs, radishes, spring onions, sweet peas and hardy annuals. Think ahead about successional sowing.

- Check all plants for signs of disease. Cut out diseased stems and flower heads and destroy.
- Hoe weekly and spread compost around growing plants.
- Feed and top-dress with compost all permanent container plants. Lightly fork the compost in.
- Plant out semi-hardy plants using a cut-down plastic milk bottle as a 'cloche'.
- Plant out sprouted potatoes. As they grow above the soil protect as necessary from frost by drawing soil over the shoots or by covering them with straw.
- 'Harden off' plants sown and grown inside.
- Water all plants recently planted and all containers inside and out. Continue to water until plants are established, and longer in dry weather.

Midsummer

- Transplant the last of the seedling brassicas and leeks.
- Sow outside lettuce, beetroot, swedes, turnip, spinach, chicory and perennial flowering plants.
- Harvest, eat and preserve ripe fruits and vegetables.
- Hoe and water plants recently planted out and sown seedlings. Keep watering pot-grown plants two or three times daily, depending on weather.
- Harvest and store ripe fruits and vegetables. Dry peas and beans for use in the kitchen and for planting next year. Dry and freeze herbs. Hang onions and garlic in bunches to dry in the sun. Use or store early potatoes and so free the ground for sowing or planting.
- Give liquid feed to growing plants and to all pot plants every week.
- Spray maincrop potatoes with Bordeaux Mixture to kill the fungus causing 'blight' if the weather is humid and still.

Late Summer

- Plant early potatoes in pots inside in order to have potatoes for Christmas.
- Turn the compost heap.
- Sow winter lettuce, winter spinach and spring onions.

References and Further Reading

Aesop, *The Fables of Aesop* (The Folio Society, 1998)

Barker, Cicely Mary, *The Little Book of Old Rhymes* (Blackie, 1976)

Buchan, Anne and Yorks, Mary, *Practical Cookery the electric way* (Alexander Hamilton, no date)

Edgar Watts Catalogue, *Ornamental and Forestry Willows and Poplar*, Willow Works, Bungay, Suffolk, NR35 1BW

Evelyn, John, *Silva: or, a Discourse of Forest Trees* (Stobart Davies Ltd, 1979)

Fellows, Miranda, *The Art of Angels and Cherubs* (Penguin Book Service Ltd, 1995)

Flowerdew, Bob, *Bob Flowerdew's Complete Fruit Book: A Definitive Sourcebook to Growing, Harvesting and Cooking Fruit* (Kyle Cathie Ltd, 2000)

Flowerdew, Bob, *Bob Flowerdew's Organic Bible: Successful Gardening the Natural Way* (Kyle Cathie Ltd, 2003)

Flowerdew, Bob and Hurst, Jacqui, *Bob Flowerdew's Complete Book of Companion Gardening* (Kyle Cathie, 2004)

Grigson, Geoffrey, *The Englishman's Flora* (Dent and Sons, 1998)

Grubb, Nancy, *Angels in Art* (Abbeville Press, 1995)

HDRA, *Catalogue of Potato Varieties*, Garden Organic, Ryton Organic Gardens, Coventry, Warwickshire, CV8 3LG

Hills, Laurence D, *Fertility Gardening* (David & Charles, 1981)

Hollis, Jill (ed), *Come into the Garden* (Ebury Press, 1992)

Hyams, Edward, *Soil and Civilisation* (Thames and Hudson Ltd, 1952)

Kipling, Rudyard, *Just So Stories* (MacMillan and Co Ltd, 1955)

Lindsay, Joyce and Maurice, *A Pleasure of Gardens* (Aberdeen University Press, 1991)

Mabey, Richard, *Food for Free* (Collins, 2001)

Morgenstern, Christian, *Gedichte* (Sulamith Wuelfing Verlag, no date)

The Organic Gardening Catalogue, Riverdene, Moleley Road, Hersham, Surrey, KT12 4RG

Seymour, John and Sally, *Self Sufficiency* (Faber and Faber, 1973)

Stuart, Muriel, *In the Orchard*, (Kettillonia 2000)

Vickery, Dr M, *Gardening for Butterflies* (British Butterfly Conservation Society, 1998)

Warner, John, *Living Willow Sculpture* (Search Press, 2003)

Werner, June (ed), *The Tall Book of Make Believe* (HarperCollins, 1992)

Index

About the Author

Beatrys Lockie was born in Holland but has lived for 55 years in Scotland with her Scottish husband. Their five children all went to the Edinburgh Rudolf Steiner School where she was a class teacher. For ten years she ran two kindergartens in south-east Scotland and lectured widely on early years education. Gardening has been her passion since childhood. She now tends an organic garden in the Scottish borders which she opens each year to the public to raise money for charity.

Other Books from Hawthorn Press

Gardening for Life – The Biodynamic Way

MARIA THUN

A practical introduction to a revolutionary art of sowing, planting and harvesting. Here are tips on favourable times for planting, harvesting and growing; ways of combating pests and diseases; building soil fertility – crop changes and rotation; how planets and stars affect plant growth.

128pp; 212 x 160mm; 978-1-869890-32-2; pb

Knitted Animals

ANNE-DORTHE GRIGAFF

Over 20 irresistible projects for making soft knitted animals. Each project is clearly illustrated with beautiful colour photographs and step-by-step instructions. Many of the animals can be quickly and cheaply knitted with small oddments of wool, and completed in an hour or two. The finished designs make enchanting children's toys, decorations for the nature or seasonal table, gifts, and articles for school fairs and raffles.

64pp; 200 x 210mm; 978-1-903458-68-6; hb

The Singing Year

CANDY VERNEY

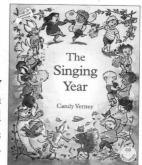

The *Singing Year* follows a child's journey through the cycle of the seasons with an exuberant collection of music, songs and poems. Each season includes ideas for activities to accompany the songs: plants for the family garden, and games and crafts using nature's bounty. For the non-musical, there are plenty of practical hints and techniques to build your confidence as a singer, and a CD so that you can hear all the songs in action.

160pp; 250 x 200mm; 978-1-903458-39-6; pb/CD

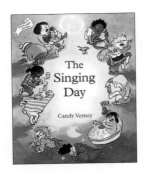

The Singing Day

CANDY VERNEY

Singing with babies is one of the joys of being a parent. It is a lifetime gift from you that children love. This easy to use songbook and CD offer practical help for singing with young children from birth to 4 years old.

160pp; 250 x 200mm; 978-1-903458-25-0; pb/CD

Getting in touch with Hawthorn Press

What are your pressing questions about the early years?

The Hawthorn Early Years Series arises from parents' and educators' pressing questions and concerns – so please contact us with your questions. These will help spark new books, workshops or festivals if there is sufficient interest. We will be delighted to hear your views on our Early Years books, how they can be improved, and what your needs are.

Visit our website for details of the Early Years Series and forthcoming books and events:

http://www.hawthornpress.com

Ordering books

If you have difficulties ordering Hawthorn Press books from a bookshop, you can order direct from:

United Kingdom

Booksource

50 Cambuslang Road, Cambuslang, Glasgow

G32 8NB

Tel: 0845 370 0063

Fax: 0845 370 0064

E-mail: orders@booksource.net

USA/North America

Steiner Books

PO Box 960, Herndon

VA 20172-0960

Tel: (800) 856 8664

Fax: (703) 661 1501

E-mail: service@steinerbooks.org

Dear Reader

If you wish to follow up your reading of this book, please tick the boxes below as appropriate, fill in your name and address and return to Hawthorn Press:

☐ Please send me a catalogue of other Hawthorn Press books.

☐ Please send me details of Early Years events and courses.

Questions I have about the Early Years are:

_____

_____

_____

_____

Name _____

Address _____

_____

_____

Postcode _____ Tel. no. _____

Please return to: Hawthorn Press, Hawthorn House,
1 Lansdown Lane, Stroud, Glos. GL5 1BJ, UK
or Fax (01453) 751138